A Cook's Journey to
Japan

Pork and Leek Miso Soup, recipe on page 57.

A Cook's Journey to Japan

Fish Tales and Rice Paddies | **100 Homestyle Recipes from Japanese Kitchens**

Sarah Marx Feldner

Foreword by Elizabeth Andoh
Photography by Noboru Murata
Styling by Yumi Kawachi

TUTTLE PUBLISHING
Tokyo • Rutland, Vermont • Singapore

Contents

641.5
952
FEL

FOREWORD
A Culinary Tour of Japan's Regional Cuisines

My own Japan journey began more than four decades ago in a coastal town on the island of Shikoku. Never intending to stay for very long, I was not especially interested in cooking at the time, and certainly not skilled in it. I sometimes marvel at the deep and powerful way in which Japan's food culture grabbed my attention from the start. In fact, it still won't let go. I remain inquisitive, asking improbable questions that often perplex the storekeepers I query and their customers with whom I chat as I peek into their shopping carts. Over the years, the roles of student-teacher have blended, even reversed: I seem to be the one offering my fellow Japanese shoppers tips on selecting the best bamboo shoots, or how to make a quick and thrifty pickle with carrot and radish peels. And I am the one who has made a career out of teaching the Japanese culinary arts, taking pleasure in kindling interest in others, helping them fan and stoke the flames of their curiosity.

Although I am firmly committed to mentoring the next generation, I am not able to work with everyone who approaches me. When Sarah Marx Feldner first contacted me in January of 2005, I was putting the finishes touches on my fourth cookbook, *Washoku: Recipes from the Japanese Home Kitchen*. Sarah said she had an idea for a cookbook of her own . . . not just a collection of recipes, but stories about the people who cooked these dishes and how she had met them while living and working as a teacher in rural Japan. Sarah wanted to provide instruction on how to recreate homestyle dishes as a way of encouraging others to explore new foods, getting them to join her on a journey of discovery beyond their daily routine. Struggling in my own way with *Washoku* to give voice to Japan's home cooking, Sarah's project excited me. Her passion of purpose (abundant enthusiasm is needed to complete such an ambitious project) and commitment to "doing it right" (no haphazard shortcuts) impressed me . . . so did her story and her desire to share it with others.

Sarah has energetically collected recipes from the kitchens and hearts of Japanese home cooks she met in her travels. Less concerned with teaching you to make dishes that boast of deep history than introducing you to contemporary fare, Sarah shows you home cooking as it is enjoyed today in busy, thrift-conscious households throughout the Japanese archipelago. Many of these, like Chicken 'n Rice Stew (Keihan)—a tasty broth-stewed chicken—enjoyed in southern Kyushu, Soy Sauce Marinated Fava Beans (Shoyumame), a specialty of Shikoku, or Vegetable-Stuffed Rolls (Oyaki) hailing from Nagano, will provide you with a culinary tour of Japanese regional cuisine in the comfort and familiar surroundings of your own kitchen. Others, like Japanese Egg Salad Sandwiches and White Radish Salad served with *mentaiko*-mayo (a salad dressing made with spicy cod roe) are relatively new to Japan but already are classics-in-the-making (in fact, mayonnaise is rapidly becoming indispensable in the modern Japanese home kitchen).

Although Sarah's journey and my own were started decades apart and in very different parts of Japan, there are many similarities. Learning through observation, a fondness for note taking, tenacious trial and error, and insatiable curiosity is our common methodology. Sharing our experiences with a wider audience, wanting to inform as we entertain others, is our common goal.

Dozo, meshiagre! (Go ahead, dig in!) Sarah will guide you well . . .

Elizabeth Andoh
Tokyo & Osaka, July 28, 2009

Rice-Stuffed Marinated Tofu Pockets, recipe on page 39.

Yakitori Chicken Skewers, recipe on page 98.

Introduction
A Search for Everyday Recipes and the Stories that Inspire Them

You could say this book arose out of desperation.

I had what most would consider a good life—a job at a growing food magazine and an adorable bungalow (with a kitchen that had been recently remodeled and featured in a national magazine!). But for me, it was simply the wrong place, wrong time.

So . . . I quit my job, sold my house, put everything I owned into storage (aka my dad's house) and returned to Japan.

About four years previous, I was graduating from college with a degree in Spanish and Applied Linguistics (Teaching English as a Second Language). And while the obvious choice would have been to go teach in a Spanish-speaking country, I, never being the one to follow too close to regimen, went to Japan instead—where it was only on the plane ride over that I first learned how to say hello (*konichiwa*) and count to three (*ichi, ni, san*).

This, though, ended up being one of the best decisions I ever made. I got a job in a lesser-known town (Iwaki) at a small, independent language school where I was one of the only Western teachers—forcing me to fully immerse myself in Japanese culture (instead of spending my time with other foreigners like myself).

Early on in my stay my sister came to visit and, one evening, I took her to Kyosaka

for dinner—one of the best restaurants in town. The restaurant's name is a combination of two famous Japanese cities—Kyoto and Osaka—and serves up some of the best *okonomiyaki* (Japanese pizza)—the Kansai region's specialty—you'll ever eat.

Again, it was meant to be. We had a cute, young woman for our waitress who had just returned from studying in Oxford, so she was able to help us with our Japanese (by speaking English). I took an immediate liking to her—it was hard not to, her smiling face just welcomed you in. My sister, knowing my tendency towards shyness, set up a lunch date for Hitomi and me a couple days later, and we have remained wonderful friends ever since! (I was there at her wedding, flew back to Japan after the birth of her first child . . .)

And really, it was her whole family that adopted me. Hiromi-san is Hitomi's aunt, and the owner of Kyosaka, who is there tirelessly cooking every night. She is also my kindred spirit. Together, the two of us can talk about food for hours . . . forever . . . which is especially impressive as she speaks very little English, and while my Japanese got better and better over time, my ability was limited. (This was a common pitfall of mine. While I—eventually—could hold my own on a discussion about Japanese food,

once the subject switched to anything non-food related, I was immediately taken out of my element, only returning a blank stare to a question that could have been as simple as "how's the weather?"—a development that always caught my conversation partner off guard).

Fast forward a couple years . . . I'm at the job with the house, along with a freshly minted master's in Library and Information Science with an emphasis on Culinary Collections and Food Research. Painfully bored, feeling scarily trapped and stuck (exactly what no twenty-eight year old wants to feel from life), I took a look at my job—where I was developing recipes, writing stories and assisting with photo shoots—and naively thought, hey, I can do this on my own, too.

And that's when I moved back to Japan with the intention of writing a Japanese cookbook.

It was a bold decision (some would probably call it "stupid"), but it's been a fun rollercoaster of a ride ever since. Looking back, I completely miscalculated the amount of time it takes to put a book of this scope together.

But I also had luck on my side. Being a librarian by education, I definitely did my fair share of research ahead of time, which is how I came across Elizabeth Andoh. While I spoke with a few other well-known

authorities in the field beforehand, it was Andoh-san who really took me under her wing. She became my mentor throughout the project, and it was beyond fortunate for me to have someone with her successful "inside" experience guiding me. (She had three books published at that time, and was in the process of putting the finishing touches on *Washoku* when we first met.) Again a sign of my cluelessness: She had told me to plan to devote four years to my cookbook project, which I ignorantly thought was crazy; that I could easily condense my time down to two years, if that. But as I sit here now, writing this introduction (one of the final steps of the book-writing process) I am at the end of my fourth year working on this book!

So I'm back in Japan . . . using Iwaki (my Japanese "hometown") as a base. Since Hitomi now had two little ones and a small apartment to house her family of four, I stayed with Hiromi-san, who lived just a few short blocks away, instead.

From there, I would go out traveling for two weeks to a month at a time, intent on speaking to whomever would talk back. And it was amazing how gracious the people I came across were: I would stay at hostels—so I could have better access to the owners and their kitchen; I would grill the volunteers at every train station tourist information center I arrived at; I enlisted the help of the Goodwill Guides (volunteer tour guides); and reached out to my extended network of Japanese "contacts" who would generously invite me into their homes, where a delicious meal and the accompanying recipe would so often be shared.

Interestingly, the more I cooked in

people's homes, the more I noticed that few would work from an actual recipe. Instead, most simply cooked "to taste." It wasn't until I was cooking with Sekia-san in Niigata that I found someone using a cookbook—of which she had photocopied the recipes she was making for me to reference. But as I took a closer look, I saw that there were no measurements provided, only a list of ingredients. When I expressed my confusion to Sekia-san, she explained that people's tastes are too varied, that it is considered an insult to tell someone, say, how much sugar to use, as the amount you might enjoy versus your neighbor's could vary greatly. (While there are definitely a large number of Japanese cookbooks out there with detailed instructions and measurements, it was this freestyle cooking philosophy I most frequently encountered.)

Throughout this entire process, I felt that I had a guardian angel (*shugotenshi*) following me around. For the most part, all of my experiences—for a girl traveling the Japanese countryside, by herself, with only a backpack and laptop strapped to her frame—were good. There were, I admit, two questionable experiences, but I was the one to blame. Like when I accepted an invitation into an older gentleman's home for lunch, who I had *just* said "hello" to on the side of the road. And shortly after entering his something-isn't-quite-right-here house and quickly realizing this was no place for me to be, I immediately made an excuse to leave, basically running out the door. Or the time I stubbornly turned down a ride back to my remote hostel, thinking I could walk the seemingly short distance back. But instead,

found myself lost in the rice paddies in the middle of nowhere in the dead of night with no idea which direction to head. Again, my guardian angel appeared. This time, in a bright red car with a friendly young woman willing to safely take me home. It was one of the only times I've hitchhiked.

Throughout the adventure (or to be more technical, my "research") I tried to stick to the smaller cities. I just felt overwhelmed by the bustle of the big cities, and found people easier to talk to—and more *willing* to talk—in the smaller rural towns.

I traveled from the northern tip of Honshu (mainland Japan—just before Hokkaido) to the southern tip of Kyushu (just before Okinawa). And it was eye-opening, that for a country roughly the size of California, how varied the cuisine is from region to region. The terrain has a lot to do with it. Whether the town is on the ocean (sea), or surrounded by mountains, has a large impact on how the people of that area eat.

In a way, this book is my small way to give something back to Japan. Having had some of my best, most memorable times there, this collection of recipes and the stories that accompany them are my way of saying "thank you" for providing the experiences that made this book possible.

Even after researching (and eating!) in Japan, and then doing more research at home in the States, I still don't consider myself an expert on Japanese food. But in a way, I think it has been to my advantage, as I am able to look at the cuisine through fresh eyes—observing techniques and ingredients that are often overlooked by those who are immersed in the food and culture.

It was also my intention to provide an introduction to Japanese cuisine that I truly felt was accessible. I love food, and I love Japan. But even for me, there are only a handful of Japanese cookbooks out there that I feel comfortable enough with to try the recipes—too often the ingredients and presentations seem too foreign or difficult. My goal with this book was to provide recipes that I—as an outside Westerner—could easily relate to. Recipes, that while still traditional Japanese, are also well within my comfort zone of both familiarity and experimentation. And traveling the countryside, in search of these recipes, I was surprised by how accessible Japanese homestyle cooking is, and how easily adaptable it is to the Western palate—and Western grocery stores.

The recipes in this book are collected from people like you: grandmothers, waitresses, fishermen, mothers, hostel owners and artists, all going about their daily lives in small mountain villages, seaside towns, and bustling cities. It is an inside peek into how these everyday people are cooking. Paging through the book, you'll quickly realize Japan is not just a country of recipes, but a country of *people* that use these recipes to feed their families, satisfy a sweet tooth and celebrate life.

You may be surprised by some of the recipes you'll find (e.g. Japanese Egg Salad Sandwiches, page 42; Oolong Tea Chiffon Cake, page 142). But just as you might try to recreate an Italian Bolognese sauce or Chinese stir-fry, these are examples of international recipes that have been given a Japanese flair by using the ingredients and

cooking methods available there. This cookbook is a combination of these traditional and "new Japanese" recipes that are a true representation of how the Japanese kitchen is evolving.

Most of the recipes included here are accompanied by a short story recounting the experience from which the recipe was collected. For me, this is an essential component to the book as I strongly believe recipes are so much more than a bunch of ingredients strung together—they're about the culture they come from, the lives of the people that prepare them.

A typical Japanese meal consists of a number of small dishes. Instead of having, say, meat, potatoes and a salad, you fill up on a selection of tiny dishes, all artistically thought through and arranged. For each dish—and the meal as a whole—there are fifteen elements, from three main categories: color (black, white, yellow, red, green), flavor (salty, sweet, sour, spicy, bitter) and cooking method (sear, simmer, fry, steam, raw). If choosing a menu that encompasses these fifteen elements, it's guaranteed to be nutritious and aesthetically balanced. This is especially true of the traditional *kaiseki* meal.

While this philosophy sounds impressive and sensible, it may also seem overly complicated and intimidating. I assure you, it isn't. I bet you'd realize you're already considering some aspect of these elements when planning your own menu (if you need some help creating a complete Japanese meal, check out the menu suggestions on page 157). But in keeping with the easy-to-relate-to nature of this cookbook, the recipes are grouped by how people typically

eat—and cook—in the West: by basic food type. That's not to say these recipes are any less traditional, they're just organized in a way that makes the most sense for the audience they are intended to reach.

One final note: Thank you for picking up this book. I sincerely mean that. Writing this cookbook has been a long, emotional process—a true labor of love. But my goal throughout it all has been to share with you the Japan I fell in love with. I hope you find the stories as interesting and the recipes as tasty as they were for me to collect.

Sarah

Sarah Marx Feldner

Useful Japanese Tools and Utensils

There are few tools unique to the Japanese kitchen that don't have a more-than-adequate, readily available Western substitute. That's great news as you should be able to prepare virtually every recipe in this book with what you already have on hand.

This is not a mere coincidence. I learned these recipes in Japanese home kitchens, and it was important to me to have that spirit easily carried on by you in *your* home kitchen (without the need for expensive, arcane gadgets or cookware).

That said, we all know that there are times when the right tool can make a job easier. Below is a list of everyday tools found in almost all Japanese home kitchens. If you wish to add any of these to your kitchen arsenal, check the Resource Guide for sources (page 157).

Bamboo sieve (Zaru) Woven bamboo sieve that comes in various shapes, sizes and depths, both bowl- and platelike. Sieves are used for any number of kitchen tasks, such as washing rice, straining noodles and drying vegetables. The flat, platelike sieves also make attractive serving platters. In most instances, a Western colander or strainer is a reliable substitute.

Cooking chopsticks (Ryoribashi or saibashi) No dexterous cook can do without these extra-long chopsticks. At first, they may take some getting used to, but in Japan, these chopsticks are the go-to kitchen utensil (hold as you would "eating chopsticks"). The long, fingerlike sticks function as if an extension of your hand. Use as you would a spoon or fork, from scrambling eggs to flipping ingredients while frying.

Cooling rack Use to cool baked goods—it allows air to circulate, preventing steam from turning the texture soggy.

Cooling racks are also very useful for draining fried foods: Simply line a baking sheet with paper towel (for easy clean up) and set a cooling rack on top. This prevents the bottom of just-fried foods from getting soggy, losing their crispy coating.

Earthenware pot (Nabe or donabe) Commonly used in winter, these Dutch oven–like pots are made of earthenware and used for making one-pot dishes called *nabemono*.

Grater, ginger This small, often ceramic dish has tiny spikes (even smaller than the Vegetable grater, see below) on a slightly raised area in the center. The spikes grate the ginger, allowing the extracted juice to pool around its diameter.

Grater, vegetable This grater has very small teeth that almost pulverize the ingredient. The box-shaped grater, as opposed to the handheld variety, is the preferred version of this tool (note: this is *not* referencing the Western "box grater"). The grater lies flat along the box below which catches the grated veggies and any juices they release. The vegetable grater is typically used for daikon (white radish), which is often added to dipping sauces, or mounded as a garnish for sashimi.

Grater, wasabi Believe it or not, wasabi does not come from a plastic squeeze bottle! The natural root is grated to reveal its deliciously pungent flavor. Traditionally, a paddle-shaped grater made of sharkskin is used, but

a vegetable grater, or the even finer ginger grater may be used in its place.

Knives (Hocho) Any well-stocked kitchen should have a good set of knives. You don't need many, but a few good ones will make the cooking process *so* much more enjoyable! With these three knives, your bases should be covered:

Vegetable knife (Nakiri bocho). Best used for vegetables, this is similar to the now popular *santokou* knife—a chef's knife with a straight edge, as opposed to rounded, so it doesn't rock.

Fish knife (Kodeba bocho). Usually about 4 inches (10 cm) long; closely resembles a mini chef's knife.

All-purpose knife (Deba bocho). Good, all-purpose knife for chicken, meat and basic fish cuts. Similar to what is referred to in the West as a "Chef's Knife."

Ladle (Otama or tamajakushi) This indispensable tool makes portioning liquid a lot easier. *Note:* Two ladles of soup should be a generous serving for one person.

Mandoline (Benriner) I've never been one to accumulate a lot of kitchen gadgets, but this mandoline is well worth the minimal clutter it adds to your drawers. Unlike many mandolines that are often a huge process just to set up, let alone decide which of the many blades to slice with, this Japanese version is a compact utensil that sets up in no time and cleans up just as easily. No matter how sharp my knife, I have never been able to shred cabbage fine enough without one.

Mortar and pestle (Suribachi and surikogi) The Japa-

Mandoline
(*Benriner*)

Cooking chopsticks
(*Saibashi*)

Omelet pan
(*Tamago-yaki-ki*)

Ladle
(*Otama*)

Slotted spoon

Wooden bowl
(*Handai*)

Rice paddle
(*Shamoji*)

Bamboo sieve
(*Zaru*)

Vegetable knife
(*Nakiri bocho*)

All-purpose knife
(*Deba bocho*)

Fish knife
(*Kodeba bocho*)

Wooden drop lid
(*Otoshi-buta*)

Mortar and pestle
(*Suribachi* and
surikogi)

Ginger grater

Wooden paddle
(*Hera*)

Wasabi grater

Vegetable
grater

nese have a very unique mortar and pestle. The inside of the bowl is lined with sharp, tiny ridges which help grind ingredients, especially sesame seeds, into a fine paste. To clean, use a stiff brush to scrape out any residue.

Omelet pan (Tamago-yaki-nabe or tamago-yaki-ki) A rolled egg is a very common dish—often served as sushi or found decorating *o-bento* (lunch boxes). It is also thinly sliced and served as a garnish (see Golden Thread Eggs, page 32). To make, beaten egg is cooked just until set and then gently rolled into a log. A normal skillet will get the job done, but this pan helps achieve that perfectly shaped roll. The best omelet pans are made of heavy copper, lined with tin.

Rice cooker (Suihan-ki) Until I actually purchased a rice cooker, I definitely would have categorized this as an "unnecessary" appliance. But as soon as I got it home, I was quickly converted. The ease with which it cooks up a perfect batch of rice is well worth the nominal investment. I've now had mine for years and use it a number of times a week. It makes cooking rice so much less of a commitment: Just wash the rice, add water, and press start . . . leaving you free to prepare the rest of the meal without a worry in sight.

Rice paddle (Shamoji) The perfect tool for fluffing and serving just-made rice, it's available in a range of materials, from wood to plastic to decorative lacquer.

Spoon, spider & slotted Always great to have on hand, a slotted spoon is especially useful when straining ingredients out of liquid—as when preparing dumplings or deep-frying

foods. If deep-frying, be sure to use a spoon made from a high-heat material, such as stainless steel.

A spider spoon is also good for deep-frying as the fine mesh is able to grab the smaller bits that break off during frying.

Strainer/fine-mesh sieve I recommend investing in a fine-mesh sieve. It's more versatile than the wider-holed colander—the small holes allow you to easily strain stocks, sift flour and drain rice.

Wok (Chuka nabe) Its high sides and deep bowl make this a great vessel for deep-frying. It's what my friend Atusko uses anytime she makes Sesame Fried Chicken (see recipe, page 95). For deep-frying, use a wok that is 14 inches (35.5 cm) or larger in diameter (see "Deep-Frying 101," page 17).

Wooden bowl (Handai or hangiri) This large, flat, wooden bowl with short sides is used for

making sushi rice—the porous wood helps soak up excess moisture. To clean, wash well with water and let air dry completely before storing. If necessary, use a *mild* soap and rinse immediately to prevent the wood from absorbing any soap flavor.

If unavailable, any large wooden bowl may be used in its place.

Wooden drop lid (Otoshi-buta) A drop lid is used to trap flavorful steam, ensure that ingredients stay submerged in their cooking liquid, and prevent delicate ingredients from breaking apart while cooking. The lids come in a range of sizes. Select one that is 1 to 2 inches (2.5 to 5 cm) *smaller* than the diameter of the cooking vessel you are using.

Before using, soak briefly in water to prevent the wood from absorbing the flavorful steam. To remove the wood odor and flavor from newly purchased drop lids, soak for 30 minutes in the milky water leftover from washing rice.

In a pinch, a sheet of aluminum foil may be used in its place. If the foil bounces a lot during cooking, place a small weight on top to help hold in place.

Wooden paddle/spatula (Hera) From stirring to sautéing to mixing, no kitchen is complete without one. I recommend having several on hand so you're not tasked with washing as you hop from one recipe to the next.

Simple Japanese Cooking Techniques

Throughout this book, a number of techniques often used in Japanese cooking are referenced. What follows are detailed how-to descriptions of these easy-to-use (and learn!) techniques.

Grating Fresh Wasabi

The easiest source of wasabi is the prepared paste found in a clear plastic tube at your local grocer. While no doubt convenient, this concoction is a far cry from the flavor of freshly grated wasabi. If you're able to get your hands on this hard-to-come-by root, by all means, use it!

1. Peel the fresh wasabi root just before using (the top part of the root is more pungent than the bottom).
2. Grate the wasabi in a slow, gentle, circular motion (this helps preserve its pungency) using a traditional sharkskin grater or fine-toothed ginger grater.

Grating Ginger and Making Ginger Juice

Ginger is found in a number of recipes in this book, often called for in grated form. Its more concentrated juice is made by squeezing freshly grated ginger.

1. Peel and grate a knob of ginger (a 3-inch/7.5-cm knob will yield about 1 tablespoon of juice). Grate the ginger using a traditional Japanese ginger grater or microplane (a ginger grater will result in a finer texture). Otherwise, the smallest side of a Western box grater will also do. Be sure to have extra ginger on hand as you lose a lot of the ginger pulp to the box grater itself. Juice will be released as you grate the ginger. To extract more juice, squeeze the pulp between your fingers.
2. For a larger quantity of juice, do as Jill Norman suggests in her gorgeously photographed book *Herbs & Spices*: Chop the ginger finely in a food processor, then wrap the shavings in a piece of cheesecloth or dish towel, squeezing the juice into a bowl.

Shaving Vegetables

This is the homestyle version of creating julienne (thin matchstick) slices of vegetables. Instead of requiring you to perfect your knife skills or break out the mandoline, home cooks that I visited simply shaved the vegetables using this whittling technique. If whittling your food seems daunting, a vegetable or julienne peeler may be used instead as the photograph below demonstrates.

1. Hold the vegetable (such as burdock or carrot) in the air at a downward 45-degree angle. Place the knife 1 to 2 inches (2.5 to 5 cm) from the bottom of the vegetable at the same angle.
2. Whittle the vegetable as you would if shaving a pencil to a point.

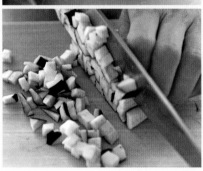

Dicing and Cubing

Dicing and cubing, a cutting technique used in kitchens in both the West and East, is used throughout this book. If you're not already familiar with how to dice or cube an ingredient, follow these easy steps. This example uses a vegetable, but other types of foods, such as firm tofu or meat, can be cut into dice or cubes as well.

1. For long vegetables like carrots or Japanese eggplant, trim the ends and then slice in half lengthwise. If the vegetable is especially thick, slice each half lengthwise again. Repeat, if necessary, to create approximately ½-inch (1.25-cm)-thick slices for cubes or ¼-inch (6-mm)-thick slices for dice.

2. Stack the vegetable slices on top of each other. Slice lengthwise to form long ½-inch (1.25-cm)-thick strips for cubes or ¼-inch (6-mm)-thick strips for dice.

3. Gather the vegetable strips together and cut crosswise into ¼-inch (6-mm) dice or ½-inch (1.25-cm) cubes.

Toasting Sesame Seeds

Although you can buy sesame seeds pre-toasted and pre-ground at larger Asian markets or online, nothing beats the flavor of freshly toasted seeds—especially when it's so easy to do yourself. For the best flavor, grind your own using a mortar and pestle—ideally, of the Japanese variety with the ribbed bowl made specifically for this purpose (see "Useful Japanese Tools and Utensils," page 12). Or, you can grind the seeds in a spice/coffee grinder.

1. Place sesame seeds in a small dry skillet. Heat over medium heat.

2. Shake the pan or stir the sesame seeds often—they are quick to burn.

3. As soon as the seeds become aromatic and turn a light golden brown, about 3 to 5 minutes, remove them from the skillet and set aside to cool. (This is important to do as the pan's carry-over heat may burn the perfectly toasted seeds.)

4. Make sure the toasted seeds are completely cooled before grinding them.

Pressing Tofu

A technique known as *mizukiri* or "water out," tofu is pressed with a small weight to remove its excess moisture. This technique is particularly useful if deep-frying tofu.

To extract water from tofu, set the tofu on a flat surface, such as a cutting board or baking sheet. Place a weight on top of the tofu for 30 minutes to 1 hour. Propping the board up at a slight angle will encourage the water to run off. Remember to set the cutting board over a sink or in a shallow dish to catch the water.

Deep-Frying 101

For as clean, healthy and simple as Japanese food is known to be, there seems to be just as many (delicious!) dishes that require deep-frying. Although I was originally quite intimidated by this technique, I quickly realized it's an easy one to pick up. Here are some of the helpful tips I learned along the way.

- If you don't have a proper deep-fryer, use a large stockpot or wok with high sides to allow for a minimum of 3 to 4 inches (7.5 to 10 cm) of headspace. This helps protect from splattering and spillovers.
- Use a neutral-flavored oil with a high smoke point, like corn, grapeseed or safflower oil.
- The oil should be a minimum of 2 to 3 inches (5 to 7.5 cm) deep.
- Although not essential, a deep-fry thermometer that clips to the side of the pot helps to ensure frying at the proper temperature. No thermometer? Test the oil's temperature by dropping in a cube of bread (it should brown in 60 seconds) or simply stick wooden chopsticks into the oil—if bubbles form, you're good to go.
- With a paper towel, pat the food dry before frying—otherwise, the excess moisture will cause the oil to dangerously bubble and rise.
- If the recipe calls for coating the

ingredients with flour or starch before frying, let the coated food rest on a wire cooling rack 20 to 30 minutes to let the coating dry and set.
- Fry in batches, so as not to crowd. This keeps the oil temperature from dropping significantly. If the oil temperature is too low, the food will absorb the oil instead of it quickly searing its exterior.
- A slotted spoon, like a wire mesh spider, is perfect for turning the ingredients while frying and then straining them from the oil.
- After frying, lay the fried food in a single layer on a wire cooling rack set over a paper towel–lined sheet pan (for easier clean up). This is especially important for foods with a coating (like starch) as it allows the excess oil to drain off while keeping the outer layer crisp. Alternatively, you can lay the fried food directly on paper towels, but the bottom of the food runs the risk of becoming unnecessarily soggy.
- For an extra-crispy coating, increase the temperature of the oil and fry a second time.
- To discard, let the oil come back to room temperature. If reusing the oil, strain through a cheesecloth, coffee filter or fine-mesh sieve and store in an airtight container. If disposing, do not pour the oil down the drain but rather throw out with the trash.

Note: *In the unlikely event of a grease fire, smother the flames with a large lid or baking sheet, pour baking soda over the flames, or use a fire extinguisher. DO NOT USE WATER.*

Chopping Vegetables for Color

This chopping technique was first taught to me by Elizabeth Andoh. Sometimes referred to as a "roll" or "oblique" cut, it is used when you want to accentuate the color of the peel, as well as create an alternatively angled version to the more traditional chop. It is often used when chopping long, narrow vegetables like eggplants and cucumbers.

1. Chop off the end of the vegetable at a 45-degree angle and discard or eat for a small snack.
2. Keeping the knife at the same 45-degree angle, rotate the vegetable a ¼-turn. Chop.
3. Repeat rotating and chopping. It's important to keep the knife at the same angle.

Essential Japanese Ingredients

My goal when writing this cookbook was to create a collection of recipes that people could relate to. Instead of looking at the ingredient list and thinking "huh?," I wanted people to say "I can make that!" And with that intention, I tried to provide recipes that, while still authentic, comprised ingredients that are more familiar in the West. Of course, what's "familiar" to some could be completely "foreign" to others. So below is a description of the commonly used ingredients in this cookbook, as well as substitute suggestions wherever applicable.

Abura-age, *see* entry for tofu.

Beefsteak/perilla (Shiso) A member of the mint family, there are two varieties of shiso.

Green shiso (*aojiso*) is often referred to as Japanese basil. The green leaf is used as a garnish, fried as tempura and served with sushi or sashimi—it's said by some to counteract the parasites in fish. Also called *oba*. If unavailable, substitute with basil.

Red shiso (*akajiso*) has a milder flavor and is used more for its color, as when pickling *umeboshi* (Japanese apricots).

Bell pepper (Piiman and shishito) Small, sweet bell pepper, the green variety of which is almost exclusively used in Japan. They are an especially popular ingredient for tempura. Shishito is the smaller of the two varieties.

Bonito fish flakes, dried (Katsuobushi) These flakes are made from bonito fish fillets that have been dried, smoked and cured until they are as hard as a piece of wood. The bonito is then shaved into beautiful, smoky fish flakes (called *katsuobushi* in Japanese). These shavings are used for a number of different culinary creations, probably most well-known for its use in Fish Stock (see recipe on page 26). Katsuobushi often comes packaged in individual 0.18-ounce (5-gram) packets. Look for it at Asian markets and large natural food stores.

Bread crumbs, Japanese (Panko) Used as a coating for fried foods, such as Breaded Pork Cutlets (see recipe on page 104). The rough-cut edges force the crumbs to lie unevenly on top of each other—creating a light, extra-flaky crust when deep fried. Used interchangeably, white

panko has had the crusts removed, while tan, or golden panko still has bits of the crust intact.

Buckwheat flour (Soba-ko) This is available at natural food stores and larger grocery stores. If desired, use white (as opposed to "whole") buckwheat flour for a milder flavor and lighter color.

Burdock (Gobo) Burdock is a root vegetable that looks like a long, brown, dirty carrot. It has a firm texture similar to a parsnip's and a flavor that's both earthy and sweet. Available year round, burdock is most commonly sold at Asian markets, large supermarkets and health food stores (it's high in fiber and vitamin B). Store in the refrigerator sealed in plastic, or wrap in paper and store as you would potatoes—in a cool, dry place. Before using, trim off any "hairs" that may be growing on the root and scrub off the outer layer of dirt with a potato brush or old washcloth—there's no need to peel the flavorful skin unless it appears unappetizingly tough. Once cleaned and portioned, immediately place the root in cold, lightly salted or acidulated water (vinegar or lemon juice work great) until ready to cook. This prevents discoloring as well as removes some of the root's naturally bitter flavor.

Cabbage, Napa or Chinese (Hakusai) Cabbage is one of the most popular vegetables in Japanese cuisine. It's often served finely shredded as a salad, pickled, or added at the last minute to hot soups to preserve its delicate flavor. Before use, cut in half lengthwise and wash thoroughly between the leaves. It can be stored tightly wrapped in the refrigerator for up to 1 week.

Chrysanthemum leaves (Shungiku) These are leaves from the chrysanthemum vegetable (not flower). They have a strong herbal—almost floral—aroma and are most commonly used in Japanese hotpots. The leaves turn bright green when cooked while maintaining their firm texture.

Cucumber, Japanese (Kyuri) Compared to the Western cucumber, Japanese cucumbers are smaller, have a thinner skin, and very small, tender seeds, if any. If unable to find Japanese cucumbers, substitute baby cucumber, English (hothouse) cucumber, or peeled and seeded Western cucumber.

Morokyu is a popular and simple snack—especially in summer—in which cucumber sticks are dipped into miso and noshed on.

Daikon Sometimes referred to as a Japanese radish or white radish, daikon looks like a large white carrot. It can be eaten raw as a snack or in salads. When cooked, it holds its shape well, making it an ideal ingredient for slow-cooked soups.

Dashi, *see* entry for fish stock.

Edamame, *see* entry for soybeans.

Eggplant, Japanese (Nasu) There are a number of different varieties of eggplant available, but on the whole, Japanese eggplants are smaller and have a thinner, more tender skin. When purchasing, look for a smooth skin and firm texture. If the stem is still intact, it should be green and fresh-looking, not withered. If unable to find the smaller Japanese eggplant, substitute with the larger Western variety but peel and seed before use. Unless being pickled, Japanese eggplants are almost never salted before using (a common technique in Western preparation).

Fava beans (Soramame) Fresh fava beans, also called broad beans, are available in the spring. Look for them at your local Asian or farmer's market or gourmet grocer. Shucked favas are available all year in the freezer section of most grocery stores. *Edamame* (soybeans) are an ac-

Chrysanthemum leaves
(*Shungiku*)

Burdock
(*Gobo*)

Japanese eggplant
(*Nasu*)

Wasabi

Mizuna

Taro root
(*Satoimo*)

Pumpkin
(*Kabocha*)

Fava beans
(Fresh, *soramame*)

Fava beans
(Dried, *soramame*)

Myoga

Bell pepper
(*Piiman*)

Garlic
(*Ninniku*)

Japanese cucumber
(*Kyuri*)

Yuzu

Lotus root
(*Renkon*)

Sudachi

Welsh onion
(*Negi*)

White radish (Daikon)

Instant dashi powder

Rice (Short-grain white)

Rice (Short-grain brown)

Rice (Black)

Soy sauce (Dark, *koikuchi shoyu*)

White miso (*Shiro miso*)

Soybean miso (*Hacho miso*)

Yellow miso (*Shinshu miso*)

Red pickled ginger (*Beni shoga*)

Soy sauce (Light, *usukuchi shoyu*)

ceptable substitute and are generally preferable to canned fava beans. In the Kansai Region (Kyoto, Osaka, Kobe), fava beans are called *otafukumame*, opposed to the more universal *soramame*. Instructions for preparing fresh fava beans can be found on page 59. Dried fava beans (used to make Soy Sauce Marinated Fava Beans, page 138) are greenish-brown with a large, flat surface and a thin black slit at the top. Also popular in Mediterranean cuisine, look for them at large Italian markets, as well.

Fish stock (Dashi) Dashi fish stock is the basis for many Japanese dishes, like miso soup. It is typically made with three simple ingredients: bonito fish flakes (katsuobushi), konbu seaweed and water. In addition, there are vegetarian versions made with only seaweed or shiitake mushrooms, as well as a version made with tiny sardines (*iriko*) (see Somen Noodle Miso Soup, page 68).

    Instant dashi powder. A convenience option for when no fresh-made stock is on hand. Although not ideal, think of this shortcut as you would a bouillon cube—there are times when an instant chicken flavor will do, and others when the rich, hearty flavor of a homemade chicken stock is essential to the dish. Similar in use to a bouillon cube, it consists of tiny pellets measured by the teaspoonful. Use according to packaged instructions, but a typical ratio is 1 teaspoon instant dashi powder per 3 cups water. Instant dashi powder is also added in small amounts to sauces as a flavoring. Ajinomoto is a common brand.

Garlic (Ninniku) Garlic is rarely used in traditional Japanese dishes, but it's still widely available throughout the country, sometimes added to sauces for dipping, for example.

Garlic chives (Nira) Although available year round, garlic chives are the most tender if harvested in the spring; they get tougher as the year progresses. Garlic chives (also called Chinese chives) have long, flat (not hollow) grasslike leaves and a stronger, more garlicky flavor than normal (hollow) chives. Do not confuse garlic chives with flowering chives whose stiff stalks require a longer cooking time. If garlic chives are unavailable, normal chives may be substituted but increase the amount used by about half, or to taste.

Ginger (Shoga) Ginger is often served with fish to help mask the odors. Grated, it's a common addition to tempura dipping sauce. To peel, scrape off the skin with the back of a spoon or paring knife. This method is preferred over a vegetable peeler as it keeps more of the ginger flesh intact. Choose ginger that is firm and heavy with an unwrinkled skin. Store in a cool, dry spot away from direct sunlight for up to 1 week. For longer storage, keep in the refrigerator's vegetable crisper wrapped in paper towels to absorb moisture, which can cause mold.

Young or baby ginger (shin shoga). It has a more delicate flavor and tender texture than mature ginger and is often used for making Pickled Ginger (see recipe on page 30). Its thin, cream-colored skin requires no peeling.

Ginger juice. See "Simple Japanese Cooking Techniques" (page 15) for instructions on how to extract ginger juice from freshly grated ginger.

Red pickled ginger slivers (beni shoga). Slivered ginger that has been preserved in salt, and then vinegar. Its bright fuchsia color is now often the result of dye, but traditionally was obtained from the natural dye of red *shiso* (perilla) leaves. Often used as a garnish.

Thinly sliced pickled ginger (gari). Pale pink in color, it is commonly served as a condiment to sushi to aid in digestion.

Myoga. Although a type of ginger, it is unique in that only the bud and stem are eaten, not the actual rhizome. *Myoga* has a very strong herbal—almost floral—aroma and flavor with a delicate crunchy texture. It is commonly used for dipping sauces and as a garnish to sashimi or other fish dishes. To prepare, clean myoga like you would a leek (slicing in half lengthwise and letting cool water run between its leaves). To help mellow its sharpness, blanch myoga before using, if desired. Its aroma will fade in the refrigerator, so store at room temperature and use as soon as possible.

Kelp (Konbu) This variety of dried seaweed is an essential ingredient for making Fish Stock, see page 26. It's rich in natural MSG. Lightly wipe with a damp paper towel before using, but don't wipe off the white powder—this naturally occurring substance contains much of the seaweed's flavor. An unopened package, stored in a cool, dry place, will keep for several months.

Lotus root (Renkon) Beige in color, it has a tough outer skin that needs to be peeled. Inside is a crisp, watery flesh. Once peeled and sliced, immediately place in acidulated water to prevent discoloration. For the same reason, only cook in stainless steel or enamel pans. Lotus root is greatly appreciated for its delicious crunch and patterned interior—when cut crosswise, a pretty flowerlike shape is revealed. If unavailable, water chestnuts make an adequate substitute.

Mayonnaise, Japanese Whether it seems traditional or not, mayonnaise is a very popular ingredient in Japan—often used in salads or as a condiment. Although tangier than American mayo, the two can be used interchangeably. Japanese mayo is now widely available at Asian markets and even large grocery stores (Kewpie is a common brand). To make a fairly accurate homemade version, combine 2 tablespoons Western-style mayonnaise with ½ teaspoon rice wine vinegar.

Mentaiko, *see* entry for spicy salted cod roe.

Mirin Made from glutinous (sticky) rice, saké (distilled alcohol), *koji* (a culture) and sugar, mirin is a sweet, syrupy liquid used to add a subtle sweetness and sheen to a dish.

Miso A protein-rich fermented soybean paste, miso is one of the oldest traditional Japanese ingredients. It is the base of miso soup—a staple of the Japanese diet, as well as a flavoring agent for any number of dishes, such as Miso-Slathered Daikon (see recipe on page 129). Among the many varieties, the basic categories are rice miso (made from rice,

Kelp (Konbu)

Dried bonito fish flakes (Katsuobushi)

soybeans and salt), barley miso (made from barley, soybeans and salt) and soybean miso (made from just soybeans and salt). Miso varies in color (from soft cream to deep, dark brown) and texture (from creamy and smooth to thick and chunky). While a few varieties have specific uses, most are all-purpose and meant to be experimented with. *Awase miso* is the art of combining different miso to find that perfect flavor for a dish, or for your family's personal taste preferences.

Soybean miso (Hacho miso). A very thick, dark, molelike miso (with hints of chocolate) made purely from soybeans. I like the Eden Foods brand that's available at natural foods stores or in the natural foods sections of some grocery stores.

Red miso (Aka miso). Light red to deep brown in color, this is a common, everyday rice miso with a high salt content.

White miso (Shiro miso). The sweetest and most

delicate variety of miso, it is a specialty of Kyoto. Expensive and often considered "high class."

Yellow miso (Shinshu miso). A good all-purpose, less-expensive miso widely available in the United States.

Barley miso (Mugi miso) A chunky miso with pieces of barley still noticeable.

Mizuna A Japanese green with a peppery bite. Often used in salads or as a garnish. If unavailable, substitute with arugula.

Mushrooms, dried Tree (Kikurage). Also known as black fungus, cloud ear, wood ear, or Jew's ear. With almost no flavor of its own, the mushroom is appreciated more for its chewy, yet crunchy texture.

Shiitake (Hoshi shiitake). In their dried state, the flavor and aroma are greatly intensified, making a deliciously meaty stock. The reconstituted mushrooms are used in many rice and noodle dishes.

Mushrooms, fresh Enoki/Enokitake. Cluster of white mushrooms with long, thin stems and small button tops. Delicate and slightly crunchy, they are either added at the end of cooking or served raw in salads.

Eringi. Also called "king trumpet" or "king oyster" mushrooms. With a thick, edible stem, these mushrooms are meaty and delicious—especially when sautéed in butter and garlic and then dipped in mayonnaise.

Hen of the woods (Maitake). These rich, earthy mushrooms grow in clumps with feathery mushroom tops. To clean, plunge quickly in water and then roll in a paper towel to dry.

Shiitake. Fresh shiitake have a much more subtle flavor than their dried counterpart. Before using, remove the tough stems (discard or save for another use, like stock). Shiitake are often used for tempura, or lightly brushed with oil and grilled.

Beech (Shimeji/Honshimeji). Similar in appearance to enoki, but with a thicker stem and larger button top that is more brown than white. *Shimeji* have a delicate texture and flavor. When buying shimeji mushrooms, be aware that they are often labeled as *honshimeji*. According to *A Dictionary of*

Japanese Food by Richard Hosking, the saying goes: "*matsutake* is for aroma, *shimeji* for flavor."

Mustard, prepared Japanese (Karashi) Japanese mustard is hotter than Western varieties as it is a blend of ground mustard seeds without the addition of flour. It's typically sold in small squeeze tubes—similar to wasabi—but with yellow tops, as opposed to green. Also found in powder form which needs to be reconstituted in water. If unavailable, hot "Chinese" mustard or Colman's mustard—either prepared or reconstituted powder form—are adequate substitutes.

Myoga, *see* entry for ginger.

Noodles, dried Soba. Buckwheat noodles. Made from buckwheat flour, with wheat flour often mixed in. Sometimes green tea is added, turning the otherwise brown noodles green. Cold soba is often eaten in summer served on a bamboo tray with dipping sauce.

Somen. Very thin wheat-flour noodles typically served cold with a dipping sauce. Cook very quickly.

Udon. Thick wheat-flour noodles often served in soups.

Chuka soba (Ramen). Thin, squiggly Chinese noodles.

Noodles, fresh Udon. Available in the refrigerator or frozen sections of large Asian markets, often sold with small flavoring packets for making *Yaki Udon*.

Soba. Available in the refrigerator or frozen sections of large Asian markets, often sold with small flavoring packets for making *Yaki Soba*.

Nori Whole, paper-thin sheets are used for, among other things, wrapping sushi and *onigiri* (rice balls). Slivered, it makes a great garnish on salads and rice dishes. (You can purchase nori pre-slivered, or make your own: use kitchen shears to cut the larger sheets into thin strips.) If the sheets are not pre-toasted (which brings out the ocean aroma and crisps the texture), toast before using by holding over a heat source for a few seconds. When rolling sushi, be sure to place the shiny side down—so the non-shiny side is facing up,

ready to be topped with rice. Store in an airtight container or it will quickly lose its crispness, becoming unappetizingly chewy.

Oil Use a neutral-flavored oil like canola or safflower. Many chefs and home cooks like to blend oils to make their own personal concoction. Hiromi-san, for example, mixes half safflower oil with half white sesame oil.

Panko, *see* entry for bread crumbs.

Potato starch (Katakuriko) This fine white powder creates a whisper-light coating on deep-fried foods. Cornstarch and the more traditional *kuzu* (kudzu) are recommended substitutes.

Pumpkin, Japanese (Kabocha) Much smaller than western squash varieties, it has a dark green skin with sweet yellow-orange flesh. Thinly sliced, it's a very popular ingredient for tempura. As with Western pumpkins, the seeds can be roasted and eaten as a snack.

Rice (Kome/Gohan) In Japan, white, short-grain rice is served with almost every meal. It is often labeled as "sushi-grade" in stores, referring more to its grain size than its limited use for sushi. Rice that has been harvested, but not yet cooked is called *kome*, while rice that has been cooked and is about to be eaten is referred to as *gohan*, or the more informal *meshi* meaning "meal." Store in an airtight container in a cool, dry, dark place. One cup (220 g) uncooked rice yields about three cups (525 g) cooked. For general rice-making guidance, see "Rice Making 101" (page 28).

Rice wine vinegar (Su) It is available in two varieties: plain or seasoned. The recipes in this book were made with *plain* rice vinegar. As with other vinegars, add at the end of cooking to give the flavors in the dish an extra "pop."

Saké (Rice wine) Although typically referred to as rice "wine," that's not entirely correct as saké is actually produced by *brewing*. In the kitchen, saké has a myriad of uses. As with wine used in Western recipes, don't cook with a saké you wouldn't want to also drink.

Hen of the woods
(*Maitake*)

Eringi

Beech (*Shimeji*)

Enoki

Shiitake
(Fresh)

Shiitake
(Dried)

Sardines, small dried (Chirimen or shirasuboshi)
These are very small sardines that have been boiled and dried. They are used as a garnish on salads or mixed in with rice. Often sold in the freezer section of large Asian markets. Once home, store in the refrigerator or freeze for prolonged storage. As stated in *A Dictionary of Japanese Food* by Richard Hosking, *chirimen* is used in western Japan; *shirasuboshi* is used in eastern Japan.

Sesame seeds, black and white (Goma) Black sesame seeds are *not* unshelled white sesame; they're just that, black sesame seeds. Compared to the white variety, they have a stronger, almost peppery flavor. Look for both black and white sesame seeds at your local grocer, health food store, specialty spice merchant, or Asian market (usually the cheapest option). Store in an airtight container placed in a cool, dry place (or keep in the freezer for prolonged storage). See "Toasting Sesame Seeds" on page 16 for instructions on how to toast sesame seeds and grind them.

Shichimi togarashi (or Nanami togarashi) A spice blend consisting of at least seven ingredients, often including *togarashi* (chili pepper), *sansho* (Japanese pepper), dried citrus zest (such as *yuzu* or *mikan*), black sesame seeds, white sesame seeds, poppy seeds and *ao-nori* (a type of dried seaweed). At traditional shichimi togarashi shops, you can choose the amount of each ingredient to suit your personal preference. Plain chili powder without the additional spices is called *ichimi togarashi* (*ichi* meaning one.) If unavailable, cayenne can be used in its place, but use less as its heat is not buffered by the additional ingredients.

Shirataki konnyaku The English translation is almost as nonsensical as its Japanese name: "Elephant Foot" or "Devil's Tongue." *Konnyaku* is a gelatinous product made from the root of the plant of the same name. Available in black (unrefined) or white (refined), it is either shaped into tofulike blocks, or thin noodlelike strands, called *shirataki*. Although flavorless, it adds texture to dishes and is praised for its nutritional properties. Look for it in the refrigerator section of large Asian markets. It should be blanched before using.

Shishito, *see* entry for bell pepper.

Shiso, *see* entry for beefsteak/perilla.

Soybeans, fresh (Edamame) Fresh, tender soybeans encased in green, furry pods. Most commonly served boiled and lightly salted with a glass of cold beer. Available fresh from summer to early autumn. Edamame are available all year in the frozen section of larger grocery stores and Asian markets—still in their pod, or already shucked.

Soy milk (Tonyu) For cooking purposes be sure to use the plain, unsweetened variety.

Soy sauce (Shoyu) Among its many uses, soy sauce is favored for marinating vegetables, flavoring soups and dipping sushi.

Koikuchi shoyu. This heavy, or dark, soy sauce is the most common, all-purpose variety of soy sauce in Japan and the US. It is used both at the table as a condiment and for making sauces, such as teriyaki.

Usukuchi shoyu. Light, or thin, soy sauce named for its color, not its sodium content (which is actually higher than koikuchi shoyu). It's the recommended variety when adding to clear broths since it won't impart as deep of a color as "normal" soy sauce. It is particularly popular in southern areas of Japan. Look for usukuchi shoyu at large Asian markets.

Tamari shoyu. This soy sauce is made without wheat. It pairs particularly well with sashimi.

Spicy salted cod roe (Karashimentaiko) A specialty of the Hakata region of Kyushu, it can generally be used whenever *mentaiko* is called for if a spicy version of a dish is desired. If unable to find *karashimentaiko*, try mixing mentaiko with 1 teaspoon of Sriracha or other hot sauce. Instructions for preparing karashimentaiko can be found on page 50.

Mentaiko. Salted cod roe. The unspiced cousin of karashimentaiko. Red coloring is often added to make mentaiko look more attractive. If possible, purchase mentaiko with no added color.

Tarako. Cod's roe. Sometimes used as a synonym for mentaiko.

Sudachi This Japanese citrus is about the same size as a lime. It has a green skin and pale yellow flesh with large seeds. Used for its fragrant zest and tart juice, it is a key ingredient for Ponzu Sauce (see recipe on page 100).

Use lime or lemon—or a combination of the two—as a substitute.

Sugars (Sato) According to Asian food authority Bruce Cost, China first introduced a crude sugar to Japan in 754 AD, and it was used solely by the upper class for medicinal purposes. In the seventeenth century, the Dutch and Portuguese introduced their version of the sweetener. And today, Japan seems to be a hotbed for the latest and greatest creative junk food confections.

Japanese black sugar (Kuro zato). Also known as *kokuto*, kuro zato is a dark brown sugar with a strong molasses flavor. It is available granulated, or in rock-hard lumps that can be melted down into a syrup. Look for it at larger Asian markets. If unavailable, dark brown sugar is an adequate substitute.

Rock sugar (Kori zato). True to its name, kori zato comes in clear or amber-tinted rocks. It is the main sweetener used when making liqueur infusions like Japanese Apricot Liqueur (see recipe on page 152). Look for it at large Asian and Southeast Asian markets.

Taro root (Satoimo) A brown, hairy member of the potato family widely available at Latin and Asian grocery stores. Although I've never had any problems, raw taro root is said to irritate some people's skin. If necessary, use rubber gloves when peeling. Once peeled, taro root becomes slippery and slimy—leaving a soaplike residue on your hands. When cooked, taro root can take on a harmless purple-ish hue. If this happens after boiling, either leave as is or peel away the tinted areas with a vegetable peeler. If necessary, small-sized potatoes can be used as a substitute.

Tempura bits (Tenkasu) These are leftover tempura bits that break off when deep-frying

tempura. Although available in shelf-stable packages at large Asian markets, for the best flavor call your local Japanese restaurant and ask them to set some fresh bits aside for you. It'll make a world of difference.

Tofu Made of fermented bean curd, tofu is a staple in the Japanese diet. There are a number of different varieties of tofu available.

Soft tofu. Its silky texture makes it ideal for adding to soups at the end of cooking. Cook just long enough to heat through.

Firm tofu. Best for sautéing and deep-frying as it holds its shape well.

Before deep-frying tofu, or mashing to make a sauce, weigh down the block of tofu for at least 20 minutes to squeeze out the excess moisture (this is a Japanese technique called *mizukiri*, meaning "water out"). See the technique for pressing tofu on page 17.

Fried tofu sheets (Abura-age). Thin sheets of tofu that, when sliced in half and gently separated, reveal a pouch inside. The standard size sheet is approximately 3 x 5 inches (7.5 x 12.75 cm).

Among other uses, fried tofu sheets can be thinly sliced and added to soups or stuffed to make Rice-Stuffed Marinated Tofu Pockets (see recipe on page 39). Before using, roll in a paper towel to remove the excess oil.

Fried tofu blocks (Atsuage). Small solid blocks of fried tofu that are light golden brown on the outside while still white in the middle. Before using, quickly blanch in boiling water to remove the excess oil.

Wasabi Wasabi is probably best known as the bright green brain-numbing garnish served alongside sushi. (It loses its flavor when cooked which is why it's always served raw as a garnish.) Wasabi is available in paste form—sold in a plastic squeeze tube—or a powder that needs to be reconstituted before use. While tasty and convenient, these versions are usually laden with artificial fillers. Fresh wasabi root is expensive and hard to come by in the West but worth seeking out. Its flavor, while still pungent, is less harsh than the commercial varieties. If using the fresh root, peel and grate just before using—slowly grating the root helps preserve its pungency. (See how to grate on page 15.)

Udon (Fresh)

Fried tofu sheets
(Abura-age)

Yuba

Shirataki

Udon (Dry)

Konnyaku

Welsh onion (Negi) Long and thin, the Welsh onion looks like a cross between a scallion and a leek. If a recipe calls for it to be cooked, a leek is a good substitute. If the recipe calls for it to be served raw, substitute with scallions instead.

White radish, *see* entry for daikon.

Yellow pickled daikon (Takuan) This traditional Japanese pickle is made from daikon (white radish) that is dyed bright yellow. Although you can make the pickles yourself, the process is long and involved. Available at large Asian grocers—try to avoid brands with artificial coloring.

Yuba *Yuba* is the skin formed when soy milk is heated. It is also called "bean curd sheets" or "bean curd skins." Although fresh is preferred, it's also available frozen and dried. Dried yuba needs to be reconstituted before use: place in boiling water for about 5 minutes, or until soft. (Dried yuba will only soften to a certain point—it can't "over hydrate." So even if you end up soaking the yuba for, say, 30 minutes, you're still okay; it won't turn mushy.) Reconstituted dried yuba lacks the flavor of fresh yuba, but it still has the same texture and protein qualities. Frozen yuba is a newer product in the United States. It is made fresh in Asia and then shipped abroad in its frozen state. If using frozen yuba, simply thaw and it's ready to use—there's no need to reconstitute frozen yuba. While frozen yuba has some flavor, the texture is inherently mushier. Fresh yuba has a fantastic texture as well as a sweet, nutty flavor. There is no need to soak fresh yuba before use.

Yuzu Japanese citrus most often used for its aromatic zest (the dried zest is a common ingredient in *shichimi togarashi*, see page 23). Its juice can be combined with soy sauce to make Ponzu Sauce (see page 100), and it also makes a delicious sorbet.

The Basics

Fish Stock
Dashi

MAKES 7 CUPS (1.65 LITERS)

In the past, I have always shied away from recipes that called for Dashi—just as I shied away from soup recipes that called for homemade stock. I assumed that taking on an extra step would be too difficult and time consuming (an ingredient to make in addition to the actual recipe!?), and I skipped such recipes altogether. But then one day I found myself with a brand new stockpot, an extra chicken and a couple of hours to spare, and I quickly realized that making my own stock was hardly the intimidating production I had made it out to be.

By the time I braved my first attempt at a batch of Dashi, I seriously started to question my initial hesitation—making Dashi is even easier (only three ingredients!) and faster (only 5 minutes after steeping!!) than making any beef, chicken, or vegetable stock you choose to spend your Saturday morning cooking up.

Although water, reconstituted instant dashi powder, or even canned chicken or vegetable stock can all be substitutes for the sake of convenience, nothing beats the flavor of a dish prepared with homemade Dashi.

The important thing to remember when making Dashi, and what sets it apart from the traditional concept of "soup stock," is not what it *tastes* like, but rather what it *does* to the food it's cooked with that gives Dashi its charm. The sole function of the two main ingredients is to act as an extraordinary flavor additive. Think of it as natural MSG, a source of *umami*. Glutamic acid (a flavor enhancer), is released from the kelp, and the dried bonito flakes (*katsuobushi*) provide inosinic acid (another flavor enhancer).

This recipe comes from Hitomi, who adapts her version from that of Yoshiko Tatsumi's, the Japanese cooking researcher. Hitomi taught me how to avoid bitter Dashi, a common pitfall among novice Dashi makers: First, don't let the water in which the *konbu* kelp is steeping come to a boil; and, secondly, when straining the finished stock, don't squeeze any of the excess liquid from the bonito flakes.

Dashi can be made ahead of time and stored in the refrigerator in an airtight container for three to four days. When it smells sweet, it's starting to turn bad. And when it smells sour, it's time to discard and make a new batch.

> 1½ pieces konbu kelp (each full sheet is 8 x 6 in/20 x 15 cm)
> 8 cups (2 liters) water
> 4 heaping cups (40 g) dried bonito fish flakes (katsuobushi)

1. To remove any dirt or grit, lightly wipe the konbu with a damp paper towel. (Konbu has a white powder on it, a source of a lot of konbu's flavor. Use light pressure so as not to wipe it off.) Break the konbu into smaller pieces.

2. Place the water and konbu in a covered container and, for best results, let steep at room temperature for a couple of hours or overnight. If your schedule doesn't permit soaking time, use the Quick Method (see below).

3. Add the steeped water and konbu to a medium pot and place over medium heat.

4. As soon as the liquid begins to gently simmer, remove the pan from the heat. Skim off any of the foam (*aku*) that rises to the surface during heating.

5. Off heat, add the bonito flakes and soak until the flakes sink, or for about 2 to 3 minutes, whichever comes first. (If you wait too long for the flakes to sink, the Dashi will taste fishy, not smoky, like it should).

6. Immediately strain the mixture through a cheesecloth, coffee filter or fine-mesh sieve. Discard the konbu and bonito flakes left in the sieve. Or, separate out the konbu and use to make Hitomi's Rice Topping (page 30). The stock is now ready to be used in a recipe.

Quick Method *In a pot over low heat, bring the water and unsoaked konbu just to a simmer. Remove from the heat, add the dried bonito flakes and continue from step 3 onwards.*

Cooking Tip *The more bonito-to-water used, the stronger the Dashi. Thus, less overall seasoning is necessary in recipes that call for Dashi as an ingredient. This particular recipe makes a "strong" Dashi.*

Special Equipment *Cheesecloth, coffee filter or fine-mesh sieve*

Vegetarian Stock
Konbu Dashi

MAKES ABOUT 4 CUPS (1 LITER)

Like the Shiitake Mushroom Stock (see right), this version is unique in that it is never heated in its preparation. As Shizuo Tsuji states in his classic text, *Japanese Cooking: A Simple Art*, the flavor and nutrients of konbu quickly pass into clear water so there is no need to subject it to heat to produce a delicate stock.

> 1½ pieces konbu kelp (each full sheet is 8 x 6 in/20 x 15 cm)
> 4 cups (1 liter) water

1. To remove any dirt or grit, lightly wipe the konbu with a damp paper towel. (Konbu has a white powder on it, a source of a lot of konbu's flavor. Use light pressure so as not to wipe it off.) Break the konbu into smaller pieces.

2. Place the water and konbu in a covered container and let steep at room temperature for 8 hours or overnight. Remove the kelp with a slotted spoon—discard, or save to make Hitomi's Rice Topping (page 30). The stock is now ready to be used in a recipe.

Cooking Tip *For a richer flavor, use this stock in place of the water when making* iriko dashi *for Somen Noodle Miso Soup (page 68).*

Shiitake Mushroom Stock
Shiitake Dashi

MAKES ABOUT 4 CUPS (1 LITER)

Like the Vegetarian Stock (see left), this version is unique in that it is never heated in its preparation (which can turn the Shiitake Mushroom Stock bitter). Instead, it is left to steep at room temperature for a few hours.

> 4 cups (1 liter) water
> 1 oz (30 g) dried shiitake mushrooms

1. Combine the water and dried mushrooms in a small bowl and let steep a minimum of 1 to 2 hours—until the mushrooms have softened and the water has turned a deep caramel-brown color.

2. Strain the mixture through a cheesecloth, coffee filter or fine-mesh sieve. (Discard the mushrooms or save for another use, such as the Marinated Mushrooms on page 31.) The strained stock is now ready to be used in a recipe.

Special Equipment Cheesecloth, coffee filter or fine-mesh sieve

White Rice Gohan

MAKES 4 CUPS (700 G) COOKED RICE

Before moving to Japan, I thought the only way to cook rice was on the stovetop. But after living in the country for a couple of months, and quickly adding rice to my daily diet, I was convinced that a rice cooker was the way to go. Of course, I was still very new to Japan at the time, and after an awkward interaction with a couple of sales clerks at the local department store, I carried home my very own mini rice cooker. Not being able to read a lick of Japanese, I stared at the instructions, trying to make out any measurements I possibly could. Turned out I didn't do the best of jobs translating as the first batch of rice I made ended up spewing out of the rice cooker and into a pool on my floor. I later learned I was trying to interpret the recipe for *okayu* (rice porridge), but even that I ended up measuring incorrectly. This story was quite the joke around the English school where I was teaching—all the Japanese mothers getting a kick out of the young foreigner learning to adapt to their culture. But adapt I did, and a few tries later I was whipping up batches of rice with the best of 'em.

I fully acknowledge that a rice cooker is not a staple appliance in most Western kitchens. And for that reason, all of the recipes in this book are prepared for the stovetop. If you do have a rice cooker at home, these recipes are easily adaptable. Just use the rice cup measure the rice cooker came with—which is equal to roughly two-thirds of a traditional dry-measure cup—and cook according to the manufacturer's instructions. For whichever preparation method used, the rice is still first prepped in the same way: rinsed, drained and left to rest (see "Rice Making 101" on this page).

2½ cups (625 ml) water
2 cups (440 g) short-grain white "sushi" rice, washed and drained (see "Rice Making 101" on this page)

1. Combine the water and rice in a 4-quart (3.75-liter) pot.
2. Bring to a boil over medium-high heat, cover tightly, reduce the heat to low, and cook for 15 minutes, or until the rice is tender and all the liquid has been absorbed.
3. Turn off the heat and let rest, with the cover still on, 10 minutes more.
4. Fluff the rice and serve.

Rice Water Tip *For extra sweetness, use the togi-jiru (starchy rice water leftover from rinsing) to boil corn on the cob. Or, you can use it to water your plants.*

Special Equipment *4-quart (3.75-liter) pot with tight-fitting lid*

Rice Making 101

• *Uncooked rice should appear almost transparent; the kernels should be whole (not broken) and clean (free of sand and dirt).*

• *Wash off the starch on the rice before using. Place the rice in a container and cover with cold water (ideally, this is the same vessel you'll be cooking the rice in). Swish the rice with your hands, being extra careful not to break the kernels—be sure to cover the rice with an ample amount of water so the kernels are not grinding against each other during washing. Carefully drain off the water and repeat. The water will start out very milky. Continue to wash and drain until the water is clear enough to count the grains of rice—usually 3 to 5 times.*

• *Drain in a fine-mesh sieve and let the rice rest in the sieve for a minimum of 30 minutes before cooking. This lets the moisture penetrate to the core of the rice kernel, yielding a fluffier, more delicious end product. When I'm in a rush—which seems to be often—I'll skip the "resting" step. The rice still turns out good, just not as good. The Japanese call this "shin-ga-nokoru," loosely translated as "half-cooked."*

• *The general water-to-rice ratio is 2½ cups (625 ml) water to 2 cups (440 g) uncooked rice. If you prefer harder rice, use less water. If using older (and subsequently drier) rice, it will absorb more water during cooking—so use a bit more. Two cups of uncooked rice should yield about four cups of cooked rice.*

Sushi Rice

MAKES 4 CUPS (750 G) RICE

There are slightly different Sushi Rice recipes in Japan—based in part on the type of vinegar used. In Kyushu's southern-most prefecture of Kagoshima, for example, you can find *saké-zushi*, sushi rice made with saké instead of vinegar.

Most sushi rice recipes include both vinegar and sugar, the sugar used, in part at least, to balance the coarseness of the vinegar. Kazuyo—my friend Ayano's mother—uses a very mild, high-quality *kome-su* (pure rice wine vinegar) which eliminates the need for a large amount of sugar.

In this recipe, the vinegar-to-rice ratio is left a little stronger to balance the sweetness of the vegetables and tofu with which it's intended to be paired (see Rice-Stuffed Marinated Tofu Pockets, page 39, and Sushi Rice with Toppings, page 81).

5 tablespoons rice wine vinegar
1½ teaspoons sugar
¾ teaspoon salt
1 recipe White Rice (page 28)

1. Whisk together the vinegar, sugar and salt in a small bowl until the sugar dissolves. Set aside.

2. Dump the hot, cooked rice into a large shallow bowl, preferably a flat wooden one. With a rice spatula or large wooden spoon, make four incisions through the rice, as if slicing a pie to form eight wedges. ("Cutting" the rice before adding the vinegar mixture allows for more even distribution.)

3. Pour the vinegar mixture into these incisions and onto the rice. Then, gently stir to combine so as not to break the rice.

Cooking Tips *It's best to use a* handai *(large, flat wooden bowl) for mixing together the rice and vinegar as the wood will absorb some of the excess vinegar mixture. If you don't have a flat wooden bowl, simply use a large shallow bowl instead.*

Be mindful of the vinegar fumes when mixing the rice. Since this vinegar is not heated beforehand (a common method for mellowing), it's still rather potent. Kazuyo had her daughter wave a paper fan over the bowl while she mixed the vinegar mixture into the rice to help disperse the fumes—a bonding experience, but not a necessary step.

Special Equipment *Handai or flat wooden bowl (see page 14)*

Hitomi's Rice Topping Furikake

MAKES ABOUT 1/3 CUP (36 G)

Furikake is a topping sprinkled over hot white rice. You can find a wide selection of premade toppings at the grocery store. But making it at home is easy, and it's a great way to use up the leftover konbu from making Fish Stock (page 26).

This dish can be prepared ahead by combining all the ingredients except the soy sauce—which should be added just before serving. If stored in a cool, dry area in an airtight container, the mixture (sans soy sauce) should last up to one week.

Konbu kelp leftover from making 1 recipe Fish Stock (page 26), rinsed clean and squeezed dry

2 tablespoons small dried sardines (chirimen), dry roasted

1 tablespoon toasted sesame seeds

1 teaspoon soy sauce

1. Preheat the oven to 300°F (150°C).
2. Spread the konbu in an even layer on a sheet pan. Bake until completely dry and shriveled, about 30 minutes. If after baking, some pieces of the konbu still feel a bit rubbery, return to the oven to finish drying, checking every 5 minutes or so.
3. Process the dried konbu in a mini food processor or spice/coffee grinder until crumbled, but not pulverized. (Don't try to use your fingers to crumble the dried konbu. The small pieces are very sharp and are prone to poke your skin.)
4. Combine the crumbled konbu, dried sardines, sesame seeds and soy sauce in a small bowl. Serve immediately over hot white rice.

Cooking Tip *You can dry roast the dried sardines and toast the sesame seeds together in the same pan.*

Special Equipment *Mini food processor or spice/coffee grinder*

Pickled Ginger Gari

MAKES ABOUT 2 CUPS (486 G)

These thin, pale-pink slices of pickled ginger are most commonly served as a condiment with sushi. *Gari* is appreciated for both its digestive qualities and ability to mask fish odors. For best results, prepare Gari using tender, young ginger (*shin shoga*), if available.

1 lb (500 g) fresh ginger root, preferably young, peeled and very thinly sliced

1 tablespoon salt

2/3 cup (160 ml) rice wine vinegar

4 tablespoons sugar

3 tablespoons saké

1 tablespoon mirin

1. Combine the ginger and salt in a small bowl and let rest 10 minutes.
2. Meanwhile, in a small saucepan, heat the vinegar, sugar, saké and mirin over medium heat until the sugar is dissolved and the mixture just starts to boil. Immediately remove from the heat and set aside. Do not let the mixture come to a full boil.
3. Squeeze the ginger with your fingers, removing as much of the liquid as you are able.
4. Place the ginger in an airtight container. Pour in the vinegar mixture, seal, and store in the refrigerator.
5. The ginger can be enjoyed after 3 days and will keep for up to 1 month.

Marinated Mushrooms

MAKES ABOUT 1½ CUPS (176 G)

These marinated shiitake mushrooms are added to many dishes—often as a garnish or tossed in with a mixture of already prepared foods. Try them in the Five Color Salad (page 48) or the Chicken 'n Rice Stew (page 82).

Served whole, they make a great finger food, and also provide the perfect vehicle for stuffing.

If a recipe calls for *sliced* Marinated Mushrooms, slice them after hydrating but before cooking.

1½ oz (40 g) dried shiitake mushrooms (about 1½ cups)

1½ tablespoons soy sauce

1 tablespoon sugar

½ teaspoon instant dashi powder

1. Place the mushrooms in a heat-proof bowl. Pour boiling water over the mushrooms, cover the bowl with plastic wrap, and let the mushrooms soak until soft, about 30 minutes. Remove the stems and discard. Reserve the soaking liquid.

2. Meanwhile, combine the soy sauce, sugar and instant dashi powder in a small bowl. Stir until the sugar is dissolved. Set aside.

3. Place the hydrated mushrooms in a small saucepan. Add 2 tablespoons of the reserved mushroom water. Stir in the soy sauce mixture—the total liquid should only come halfway up the mushrooms, not cover them entirely. Add more mushroom water, if necessary. Simmer over medium-low heat until most of the liquid has been absorbed, 10 to 15 minutes. (While simmering, skim off the bitter, white *aku*, or foam, that rises to the top as the mushrooms cook.)

4. Enjoy the mushrooms cold or at room temperature.

Golden Thread Eggs
Kinshi Tamago

MAKES 1 CUP (125 G) FROM ABOUT 3 PANCAKES

These egg threads are often used as a garnish at the end of cooking to add a pop of color to a dish (see Sushi Rice with Toppings, page 81, or Chicken 'n Rice Stew, page 82).

For uniformly yellow egg pancakes, be sure to whisk the eggs so that there is no trace of white remaining. Re-whisk the mixture before each pancake is made to ensure aesthetic consistency. Admittedly, forming perfect pancakes might take a couple of tries. But don't worry. Whether or not you shape and flip a perfect circle in no way affects the flavor. Even the "scraps" will work.

There are two easy methods for cutting the egg threads. The technique of stacking and slicing into half-moons, as my friend Atsuko taught me to do. Or, the traditional method of first folding the pancake into thirds, and then slicing. Use whichever method you prefer.

3 eggs
½ teaspoon sugar
½ teaspoon salt
Oil

1. Whisk together the eggs, sugar and salt in a medium bowl. Be sure to mix well—the eggs should appear completely yellow when cooked, with no traces of white.

2. Over low heat, lightly oil a skillet (with about 1 teaspoon oil) and pour approximately one-third of the egg mixture into the pan. Continuously rotate the pan to disperse the uncooked egg across the surface of the pan, forming a large pancake. When no more egg liquid remains, after about 1½ to 2 minutes, flip to cook the other side—use a chopstick or spatula to gently and patiently release all sides, then use both the spatula and your other hand to safely flip the pancake over. Cook 1½ to 2 minutes more.

3. Repeat with remaining egg mixture, refreshing the oil as necessary.

4. Stack the cooked "pancakes" one on top of the other. Cut in half to form a half moon, stack these on top of each other, and cut, crosswise, into thin short strips.

5. Alternatively, fold a pancake into thirds, and cut, crosswise, into thin short strips. Repeat with remaining pancakes.

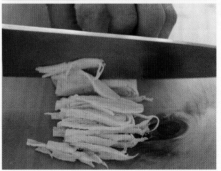

Cooking Tip *To get the proper thickness of the egg pancake, it's best to use an 8- or 10-inch (20- or 25-cm) skillet. If using a larger skillet, for each pancake, add more of the egg mixture to the pan. Smaller? Add less.*

Peanut Miso

MAKES A HEAPING ⅓ CUP (134 G)

Always the creative cook, this is another of Hitomi's delicious recipes. The sweetness of this miso sauce pairs perfectly when used as the miso filling in the Miso-Filled Rice Patties (page 78). It can even be adapted to favorite American dishes: When my good friend Sarah Buckley tested this recipe, she used the miso as a "glaze" for chicken or pork just off the bbq—or out of the oven—and loved it.

- 1½ tablespoons rice wine vinegar
- 2 tablespoons saké
- 2 tablespoons mirin
- 2 tablespoons sugar
- ¼ cup (60 g) miso (preferably red)
- ¼ cup (30 g) coarsely ground dry roasted unsalted peanuts
- Yuzu or other citrus zest, optional garnish

1. Bring the rice wine vinegar to a boil in a small saucepan over medium-high heat. Pour in the saké, mirin and sugar, stirring after each addition. Whisk in the miso. When fully incorporated, add the peanuts and whisk constantly for 1 to 2 minutes more. The sauce will be bubbly, a deep caramel color, and starting to thicken.
2. Pour into a small bowl and let cool. (The sauce will continue to thicken as it cools.) Garnish with the zest before serving, if desired.

Cooking Tips *The peanuts can be ground in a mortar and pestle, with a few pulses in a food processor, or simply chopped fine.*

The texture of the miso is up to you. I prefer it a bit chunkier and leave the peanuts on the coarser side.

Eggplant Miso Abura Miso

MAKES ABOUT 1 CUP (304 G)

This is a very quick and simple recipe that can be prepared on moment's notice—in the Japanese kitchen, these ingredients are always on hand. And this dish is exactly what my friend Mari whipped up for us after spending the day at her mother's A-frame mountain retreat outside of Nagano. After we returned to the city of Matsumoto where my friend Ayano lives and apprentices with a famous kimono maker, we huddled around a small table in the middle of Ayano's cozy living quarters drinking beer and snacking on chips. As I inquired about Vegetable-Stuffed Rolls (page 40), Mari whisked off to the kitchen to demonstrate the use of this eggplant miso as a delicious filling. The miso also makes a fast weeknight dinner simply served over a bowl of steaming rice.

- 4 tablespoons miso
- 4 teaspoons sugar
- 4 tablespoons oil
- 2 Japanese eggplants, minced

1. Stir together the miso and sugar in a small bowl. Set aside.
2. Add the oil to a skillet, preferably nonstick, and set over medium-high heat. When hot, add the eggplants and fry until translucent, cooked through, and starting to brown, about 5 minutes. Add the miso mixture and, stirring constantly, cook 1 minute more, watching carefully so as not to burn. You want the eggplant and miso mixture to become a soft, mushy sauce, each ingredient blending into the other.

A Note About Miso

In America, it's a pretty safe bet that upon opening a refrigerator one will likely find a bottle of ketchup. In Japan, you're even more likely to find a package of miso. Used for dips, salads, soups, sauces . . . even ice cream, miso is an essential ingredient when it comes to Japanese cooking. Grocery stores, in fact, devote an entire aisle to the soybean "condiment," available in an assortment of flavors and colors and from a multitude of manufacturers. So when it came time for Atsuko and I to cook together, and miso was needed, I was more than pleasantly surprised when, instead of heading towards the refrigerator, she revealed a large ceramic crock filled with homemade miso quietly fermenting underneath her kitchen sink. I was again reminded of how much I enjoy cooking with Atsuko. It's always comforting to find a cook that still makes the effort to preserve the lost arts. While frugality may have initially driven her to be so industrious, convenience is still temptingly justifiable. But she has yet to give in.

Marinated Fried Tofu Abura-age

MAKES 2 SHEETS

For all you skeptics out there, this is tofu like you've never seen it. These sweet, marinated sheets (with a surprise pocket inside) are used in one of my favorite salads in Japan, Five Color Salad (see recipe, page 48).

¼ cup (65 ml) reserved mushroom water (see Marinated Mushrooms, page 31) or water

3 tablespoons soy sauce

2 tablespoons sugar

1½ teaspoons mirin

½ teaspoon instant dashi powder

Two 3 x 5-in (7.5 x 12.75-cm) sheets fried tofu (abura-age), rolled in paper towel to remove excess oil

1. Add the water, soy sauce, sugar, mirin and instant dashi powder to a small saucepan and bring just to a boil. Add the tofu and place a piece of aluminum foil directly on the surface to help submerge the tofu in the liquid. Simmer over medium-low heat for 10 minutes, or until the tofu is tender, but not so soft it is quick to tear. Remove from the heat.

2. Let the tofu cool to the touch in the pan, then gently squeeze the excess liquid back into the pan. The liquid can be used in other recipes, like the Five Color Salad (page 48). Set the tofu aside. The marinated tofu is now ready to be used in a recipe.

Cooking Tips *To eliminate excess oil, roll the fried tofu sheets* (abura-age) *in paper towel before using.*

Traditionally, an otoshi-buta *(wooden drop lid) is used to help keep the tofu sheets submerged in the marinating liquid. But for practical purposes, I have called for a sheet of aluminum foil, instead.*

Special Equipment *Aluminum foil or wooden drop lid*

Sesame Salad Dressing

This salad dressing seems to make an appearance at every home and restaurant I visit. It's so good people will find an excuse to put in on anything! Needless to say, I knew I'd stumbled on a goldmine when Atsuko nonchalantly shared her recipe with me. Try serving this dressing with the shredded cabbage accompaniment found in the recipe for Breaded Pork Cutlets (page 104).

> 2 tablespoons toasted sesame seeds (see page 16)
> Generous ½ cup (75 g) coarsely chopped white onion
> 1 large clove garlic, coarsely chopped
> ½ cup (125 ml) soy sauce, preferably light
> ½ cup (125 ml) oil, preferably canola or other neutral-flavored oil
> ½ cup (125 ml) rice wine vinegar
> 2 tablespoons sugar
> ½ teaspoon salt
> ½ teaspoon fresh cracked white pepper

1. Grind the toasted sesame seeds in a mortar and pestle or mini food processor until powdery. Set aside.

2. Add the onion, garlic, soy sauce, oil, vinegar, sugar, salt, pepper and ground sesame seeds to a blender and process until smooth. Serve over your favorite salad.

3. Have extra? Store in an airtight container in the refrigerator for up to 2 weeks. Stir well before using.

Cooking Tip *In this recipe, "light" soy sauce is called for. This is a reference to its color, not salt or caloric content. "Regular" soy sauce is an adequate substitute (use the same amount called for in the recipe), but just be aware that the end result will be darker in color.*

Special Equipment *Mortar and pestle or mini food processor; blender*

Quick and Easy Pickles Tsukemono

These pickles were prepared as a side dish at one of the dinners I shared with Reiko at the Obuse Guide Center. Incorporating only three ingredients, I was amazed at how colorful and fresh tasting the pickles were. As so few ingredients are used, this recipe highlights—and depends upon—the quality of the vegetables' flavor. Preparing this dish is a great opportunity to use what's growing in your garden or in season at your local farmer's market. Thinly shave the carrots with a julienne peeler or sharp knife using the technique shown on page 15.

> 1 Japanese cucumber or ⅓ English (hothouse) cucumber, cut into chunks (see "Chopping Vegetables for Color," page 17), or sliced on the diagonal
> 1 small carrot, shaved (see "Shaving Vegetables," page 15) or peeled
> ½ to ¾ teaspoon salt

Combine the cucumber, carrot and salt in a small, resealable plastic bag. (If you're sensitive to salt, use ½ teaspoon of salt; if not, use the full ¾ teaspoon.) Let stand 15 minutes, occasionally gently shaking.

Cooking Tip *In place of a Japanese cucumber, an "American" garden-variety cucumber may be used—just peel the skin (unless unusually thin) and deseed.*

CHAPTER 1

Snacks and Salads

To many, it may seem like Japanese food is just one big snack—each meal comprised of a large number of small dishes. True in part, this chapter actually contains what we in the West would consider *real* snacks—mini-meals meant for nibbling before dinner, or with a bottle of beer and some good conversation. If you're having a party, many of these recipes are easily converted into appetizer favorites.

And when it comes to salads, they seem to be gaining more and more popularity in Japan. Although oftentimes served as simply a small mound of finely shredded cabbage alongside, say, a perfectly fried pork cutlet (see Breaded Pork Cutlets, recipe on page 104), green salads, with bright red cherry tomatoes and shaved strands of orange carrot, are becoming more common. But for me, any reason to eat a green salad in Japan is just an excuse to break out the Sesame Salad Dressing (page 35)!

A Cook's Journey to Japan

Rice-Stuffed Marinated Tofu Pockets Inarizushi

I n shades of white and tan, *Inarizushi* taste incredible, travel well and are favored by many. Knowing my strong preference for the little snacks, Ikuko made a huge batch for my potluck *sayonara* party when I first left Japan after teaching English for a year, and Hiromi sent me home to America with an artfully arranged *o-bento* (lunch box) full of them.

MAKES 16 POCKETS

Eight 3 x 5-in (7.5 x 12.75-cm) sheets fried tofu (abura-age), rolled in paper towel to remove excess oil

1 cup (250 ml) reserved mushroom water (see Marinated Mushrooms, page 31) or water

6 tablespoons sugar

¼ cup (65 ml) soy sauce

1 tablespoon mirin

1 teaspoon instant dashi powder

¼ cup (30 g) diced carrot

¼ cup (30 g) minced burdock or turnip

1 recipe Sushi Rice (page 29)

1 tablespoon black sesame seeds

1. Cut each fried tofu sheet in half crosswise to reveal the pockets.

2. Add the water, sugar, soy sauce, mirin and instant dashi powder to a small saucepan and bring just to a boil. Add the tofu sheets and place aluminum foil directly on the surface of the liquid to keep the tofu sheets submerged. Simmer over medium-low heat for 10 minutes, or until the tofu is *just* tender. If it becomes too soft, it is quick to tear. Remove from the heat.

3. Let the tofu cool to the touch in the pan, then gently squeeze the excess liquid back into the pan. Set the tofu aside.

4. Add the carrot and burdock or turnip to the remaining liquid in the pan and simmer over medium-low heat, uncovered, for 10 minutes. Drain any remaining liquid.

5. Combine the cooked carrot and burdock

in a large bowl with the Sushi Rice and sesame seeds.

6. Using your finger, gently open each pocket of tofu and fold the top of the tofu over to reveal the inside.

7. With damp hands, form ¼ cup (40 g) of the rice mixture into a small ball. Then gently press the rice ball into a tofu pocket, trying to fill the corners as much as possible. Fill the rest of the tofu pockets in the same way.

8. You can serve Inarizushi with the seam-side facing either up or down. Enjoy at room temperature or chilled from the refrigerator.

Cooking Tips *There are two main types of fried tofu. One has a pocket you can stuff, the other doesn't. You need a sheet of fried tofu with a pocket inside (abura-age) for this recipe.*

It is best to let the rice mixture cool before stuffing the tofu pockets. When warm, it contains additional moisture that can seep out of the rice, making the finished product soggy.

The addition of mirin not only provides a sugary taste, it also brings out the overall amami (sweetness) of the dish.

Traditionally, the abura-age is cooked with an otoshi-buta (wooden drop lid) to help keep the tofu sheets submerged in the marinating liquid. But for practical purposes, I have called for a sheet of aluminum foil, instead.

Special Equipment *Aluminum foil or wooden drop lid*

Vegetable-Stuffed Rolls Oyaki

I kuko has a relative that lives about an hour outside of Nagano in the small mountain village of Kinasa, a village famous for its Oyaki. Since the Japanese love giving gifts, and food is often the medium, it was no surprise when Ikuko received a a large box of Oyaki one day. But it *was* fortuitous that I happened to be around the day the present—dense, crispy rolls stuffed with a variety of perfectly prepared seasonal vegetables—arrived. And that's how I happened to find myself heading towards Kinasa on a decrepit local bus slowly snaking its way up the steep mountain road, inches away from high jagged cliffs on one side and a deep river gorge on the other. Not only was I the only foreigner on the bus (and, apparently, the first American to ride into Kinasa for some time—just before leaving the village the next morning, I stopped at the post office to mail a letter and, no exaggeration, it took three(!) postal employees to determine the correct postage for a normal-sized letter to America!), I was also the only person under seventy-five years old on the bus. It was charming to watch the youthful elderly passengers, obviously all regulars, happily taking their time getting off at each seemingly in-the-middle-of-nowhere stop, leisurely saying their goodbyes to the other riders, then patiently waiting along the side of the road as the bus carefully drove away, customarily bowing their extended *sayonaras* once more.

A Note About Oyaki

Oyaki is a very homestyle, very traditional snack food popular in Northern Japan, especially in the areas surrounding Nagano. In this mountainous region, where it is difficult to grow rice, cooks were required to be creative with the limited resources available: Oyaki dough is typically made from a simple combination of wheat flour and water; sometimes buckwheat flour is added as well. (Happily, Oyaki dough is very easy to work with. It requires only a minimum amount of extra flour to prevent the dough from sticking to the surface while kneading.)

The formed Oyaki rolls are then stuffed with a variety of local, seasonal ingredients such as thistle, daikon, Japanese pumpkin, rape blossoms or Nozawana (a bitter green leaf vegetable). Traditionally, Oyaki are browned "until it reaches a nice fox-color" in an houroku nabe *(baking pan) and then buried in the ash of the* irori *(sunken hearth), the trapped heat forcing the rolls to puff. Today it is not uncommon to find Oyaki that have been steamed, baked or fried.*

I have sampled my share of Oyaki and have found, like most Japanese, the ones from the famous shop, 'Irohado', in Kinasa to be the best. The recipe on this page is inspired by their inventiveness.

MAKES 8 ROLLS

- ¾ cup plus 3 tablespoons (128 g) all-purpose flour
- ½ cup (62 g) bread flour
- ½ cup (62 g) buckwheat flour
- ⅔ cup (160 ml) water
- 1½ teaspoons kosher salt
- 1 cup (304 g) Eggplant Miso (page 33), room temperature
- 1 teaspoon oil

1. Combine the all-purpose, bread and buckwheat flours in a large bowl. Pour in the water and stir just to combine. Cover the bowl with a cloth towel and let rest for 10 minutes (this helps hydrate the dough).

2. Pour the contents out onto a lightly floured work surface and knead until the dough comes together. Add the salt and continue kneading until the dough appears smooth, about 5 minutes. Return the dough to the bowl, cover the dough's surface with plastic wrap, and let rest for 30 minutes.

3. Preheat the oven to 350°F (175°C). Line a baking sheet with parchment paper.

4. Follow the illustrated steps on the opposite page for making the rolls.

5. Heat a cast-iron skillet until very hot. Add just enough oil to coat the bottom of the pan. Then, add as many rolls as will comfortably fit in the pan—seam-side down—and fry until golden, about 20 seconds. Flip to brown the other side. Place on the parchment-lined baking sheet—seam-side down—and repeat with remaining rolls. The 8 rolls should easily fit onto one baking sheet.

6. Bake the browned rolls for 20 to 25 minutes, or until browned and puffed with a hard outer crust. Remove the rolls from the baking sheet and transfer to a cooling rack. Let rest 5 minutes, or until cool enough to handle. Serve warm or at room temperature.

Special Equipment *Well-seasoned cast-iron skillet; parchment paper*

Making the Oyaki

1. *Turn the dough out onto a lightly floured work surface. Using a sharp knife or bench knife, divide the dough into 8 pieces. Cover with a cloth towel.*

2. *Using your hands or a small rolling pin, press out a piece of dough into a thin, flat circle, about 3 to 4 inches (7 to 10 cm) in diameter. (Remaining dough pieces should still be covered with the towel.)*

3. *Place 2 heaping tablespoons of the Eggplant Miso filling in the center.*

4. *Wrap the dough around the filling —as if forming a purse.*

5. *Pinch and twist the edges together to tightly seal the roll.*

Japanese Egg Salad Sandwiches

The inspiration for this recipe was passed on to Atsuko from her friend, who happened to see these colorful sandwiches while waiting for a plane at the airport on Amami-Oshima, a small island just north of Okinawa. We made a large stack of them to bring along on our afternoon picnic to Kasumigaura, the second largest lake in Japan.

These sandwiches are very pretty to look at! Once assembled and cut into small triangles, the soft white bread frames the bright yellow of the egg salad and the bold green and orange of the vegetables. Though easy to make, you do need to set aside an hour for the cucumber and carrots to marinate before assembling the sandwiches.

MAKES 3 WHOLE SANDWICHES

2 tablespoons sugar

2 tablespoons soy sauce

2 tablespoons rice wine vinegar

½ Japanese cucumber or ⅛ English (hothouse) cucumber, cut into matchsticks (about 1 cup/130 g)

1 medium carrot, peeled and cut into matchsticks (about 1 cup /130 g)

4 hard-boiled eggs, peeled and crushed

½ cup plus 2 tablespoons (125 g) mayonnaise, divided

½ teaspoon prepared hot mustard (Japanese, Chinese or Colman's)

6 slices soft, white sandwich bread

1. Mix the sugar, soy sauce and rice wine vinegar in a small bowl until the sugar has dissolved. Place the cucumber and carrot in separate dishes; divide the sauce between the two. Let marinate for 1 hour.

2. In another small bowl, combine the eggs and ¼ cup (50 g) mayonnaise. Set aside.

3. In yet another small bowl, stir together the remaining mayonnaise and Japanese mustard. Set aside.

4. To assemble the sandwiches, spread 1 tablespoon of the mayonnaise-mustard mixture on each of the 6 slices of bread.

5. Gently squeeze the marinating liquid from the cucumbers; divide the cucumbers into three portions. Place one portion of the cucumbers at a diagonal on the mayo-smeared bread, from the bottom left corner to the upper right corner. Repeat with the two other pieces of bread.

6. Gently squeeze the marinating liquid from the carrots; divide the carrots into three portions. Place one portion of the carrots at an opposite diagonal on the same slice of bread to form an "X." Repeat with the two other pieces. Place a small spoonful of the egg-mayonnaise mixture in each of the four empty triangle spaces between the veggies. Repeat with the two other pieces of bread.

7. Top each dressed sandwich half with the remaining three slices of mayo-smeared bread. Cut each sandwich into four triangular-shaped wedges to reveal the colorful vegetables.

Cooking Tip *For perfect hard-boiled eggs, place eggs in a small pot and cover with 1 inch (2.5 cm) of water. Bring to a boil. As soon as the water starts boiling, cover the pot, remove it from the heat, and let sit 10 minutes. Remove the cover and immediately flush the pot with cold water from the faucet. Once the temperature of the water has cooled, add ice cubes and let the eggs continue to cool for 20 minutes. Drain.*

Japanese Cocktail Peanuts

These peanuts are a great, salty accompaniment—noshed on by the handful—to a cold glass of beer. They were first served to me seasoned with *katsuobushi* (dried bonito fish flakes). If the addition of a smoky fish flavor feels a bit too adventurous, feel free to omit it; the peanuts will still taste fantastic. The recipe provided below is a twist on a local dish from the Amami Islands in southern Japan.

MAKES ABOUT 6 CUPS (598 G)

¼ **cup plus 2 tablespoons (108 g) miso, preferably red**

¼ **cup plus 2 tablespoons (75 g) sugar**

¼ **cup plus 2 tablespoons (48 g) sesame seeds**

1½ **teaspoons salt**

1 **lb (500 g) dry roasted, unsalted peanuts (about 3 cups)**

One 0.18-oz (5-g) packet dried bonito fish flakes (katsuobushi) (about ½ cup) (optional)

1. Preheat the oven to 300°F (150°C).
2. Combine the miso, sugar, sesame seeds and salt in a medium bowl to form a paste. Add the peanuts and stir to coat.
3. Bake the peanuts on an aluminum foil–lined baking sheet for 30 minutes, or until browned, being careful not to burn. Stir the peanuts every 10 minutes or so.
4. Immediately sprinkle the dried bonito flakes over the peanuts, if using, and stir to coat. The heat from the hot peanuts should make the fish flakes stick.
5. Transfer the peanuts to a large plate or another baking sheet—large enough for the peanuts to lay in a single layer—and let cool completely before serving. The peanuts will crisp up as they cool.
6. Store in an airtight container for up to a week; humidity will cause the peanuts to soften.

Cooking Tip *Do not substitute raw peanuts for the dry roasted, the end result will be chewier and less crisp than desired.*

Crispy Rice Snacks Okoge

Before the advent of the rice cooker, rice in Japan was made in an *okama* pot placed over an open flame. Inevitably, a thin layer of rice would stick to the bottom, slightly burnt and crispy—*okoge*. This layer was coveted by all who were dining, each hoping to get a piece with their serving of rice.

Today, Okoge, similar in popularity to the *socarrat*, or burnt rice, found at the bottom of a Spanish paella pan, has deservedly become a dish in its own right—thin rice patties are grilled over an open flame until crisp, taking on a slightly smoky flavor.

At Kyosaka, Hiromi's restaurant, Hiromi serves the Okoge seasoned with *shiso* and glazed with soy sauce. If you have access to the herb, finely slice a few shiso leaves and stir into the freshly cooked rice just before shaping into patties.

Use piping-hot rice when forming your Okoge as the steam helps the rice stick together. Before cooking, the patties are chilled for at least two hours to firm up, so remember to plan for this time. (If desired, the patties can be shaped up to a few days ahead, and then cooked just before serving.) At Kyosaka, Hiromi grills the Okoge over a small grate conveniently situated next to the *teppan* (flat iron griddle). I don't have a built-in grate on my stove, though! (And I don't expect you to either.) In trying to replicate the recipe at home, I have found that shallow-frying creates the best results.

MAKES ABOUT 16 PATTIES

1 recipe White Rice (page 28)
Oil, for frying
¼ cup (65 ml) soy sauce

1. Drop ¼ cup (40 g) of the hot, just-cooked rice onto a wax paper–lined baking sheet.

2. Using damp hands, gently press the rice to form a thin, oval patty (about 2 to 4 inches/5 to 10 cm long and between ¼ and ½ inch/6 mm and 1.25 cm thick). If the rice feels particularly sticky to you, form the patties between two sheets of wax paper.

3. Repeat with the remaining rice to form approximately 16 patties.

4. Cover with plastic wrap and chill for 2 hours, or until set. (The patty should be stiff/firm enough to be easily picked up and still retain its shape.)

5. Heat 2 to 3 tablespoons oil in a large skillet over medium-high heat—enough oil to pool slightly around the patties. Fry the chilled patties in batches so as not to crowd the pan (about 3 to 4 patties per batch), and cook until crisped and lightly browned, 3 to 5 minutes per side. (Make sure the patties have crisped up nicely before removing them from the pan; otherwise they won't hold up well once glazed with the soy sauce, falling apart when handled.) Transfer the patties to a paper towel–lined baking sheet to drain. Lightly brush the tops with the soy sauce. Repeat with remaining patties, refreshing the oil between batches. Best if served warm.

Cooking Tips *Take the amount of oil called for in this recipe loosely. The amount needed for each batch varies on the size of the pan and the number of patties being cooked. The larger the pan and the more patties being cooked at one time, the more oil that is needed to properly crisp the rice. For a 10-inch (25-cm) skillet, use 2 tablespoons oil and fry 3 to 4 rice patties per batch. (Fry just 3 patties at a time if you want the rice to be extra-crispy.)*

The rice will crisp much faster than it will brown in the oil. Most of the caramel color on the okoge *comes from the soy sauce glaze rather than browning.*

Special Equipment *Baking sheets; pastry brush; ¼-cup (65-ml) measure*

Ginger-Fried Soybeans
Daizu to Chiriman no Ageni

I love the way these beans feel in the mouth. They are crispy on the outside and soft on the inside, perfectly paired with the crunch of the sesame seeds and dried sardines. The salty/sweet ginger combo adds yet another layer of flavor. (Of course, if the dried sardines are not to your taste, simply omit them.)

This is a fun dish to eat in a communal, social setting while imbibing bottles of Japanese beer. Place a big bowl of these fried beans between a group of friends, and let them chase the beans with their chopsticks.

This recipe is quite simple to make but it does require some strategic planning. First, you need to remember to leave time for soaking and cooking the dried soybeans. (Although if you're using canned soybeans you can breeze through these steps, but I recommend using dried beans for their firmer texture.) The other key to success is to have all the ingredients prepped and prepared ahead of time, including the Ginger Sauce, so that you can immediately dress the beans when they're removed from the hot oil. This is the best way to maintain their crispy fried texture.

SERVES 6

1 cup (225 g) dried soybeans, soaked overnight, drained and rinsed, or 4 cups (1 kg) canned soybeans, drained and rinsed

Oil, for deep-frying

2 tablespoons small dried sardines (chirimen) (optional)

1 tablespoon sesame seeds

½ cup (80 g) potato starch

2 tablespoons chopped chives

½ teaspoon kosher salt, or to taste

GINGER SAUCE

2 tablespoons soy sauce

1 tablespoon sugar

½ teaspoon ginger juice (see "Making Ginger Juice", page 15)

1. If you're using dried soybeans, place the soaked and drained soybeans in a large stockpot with at least 8 cups (2 liters) of water. Bring to a boil, then turn the heat down to medium-low and simmer for 3 hours, or until soft. (You may need to add additional water to the pot while the beans are cooking.) Drain. You should have 4 cups (1 kg) of cooked soybeans.

2. To make the Ginger Sauce, whisk together the ingredients in a small bowl until the sugar is dissolved. Set aside.

3. Pour 1 tablespoon of oil into a small skillet, over medium-high heat. Add the dried sardines and sesame seeds and fry until golden, 2 to 3 minutes. Pour onto a paper towel–lined plate to drain and cool. Set aside.

4. Add a minimum of 2 inches (5 cm) of oil to a deep-fryer, large wok or stockpot and heat to 350°F (175°C).

5. While the oil is heating, pat the soybeans dry with paper towels.

6. Toss the soybeans with the potato starch in a large bowl until evenly but lightly coated; shake off any extra starch. Fry the coated beans, in batches so as not to crowd, until golden and crispy, about 3 minutes. Remove the beans with a slotted spoon and place them on a paper towel–lined platter to remove the excess oil. (As you fry the beans in batches, keep the just-fried beans in a single layer until completely cool—this helps them retain their crispy coating.) Repeat with the remaining beans.

7. Combine the fried beans, sardine mixture, chives and salt in a large bowl. Drizzle the Ginger Sauce over the top, toss gently and serve.

Cooking Tips *When frying the beans, be careful not to add too many beans at once or the oil temperature will drop drastically. Also, the moisture in the beans will cause the oil to bubble and rise. Be sure to fry in a deep enough pot to ensure that the hot oil does not boil over.*

See "Deep-Frying 101" on page 17 for more tips.

Five Color Salad Goshiki-ae

With *go* meaning "five," and *shiki* meaning "color," the name of this recipe represents the colors of each of the main ingredients used. All the "work" that goes into making this salad comes from preparing each of the five ingredients, all of which—besides the salted cucumbers—can be done ahead of time. The actual colors featured in the dish will vary depending on the creativity of the chef and the availability of ingredients. I learned how to make *Goshiki-ae* from Ms. Banzai, whose welcoming home is in the middle of farmland, surrounded by the jagged snow-capped mountains of Niigata.

Just before serving the salad, Ms. Banzai tasted the salad's seasoning. Not completely satisfied, she opened the fridge and decided upon the mustard. The perfect choice: with just a few drops it effortlessly enhanced the flavor from good to great.

SERVES 6 TO 8

½ cup (70 g) thinly sliced Japanese or English (hothouse) cucumber

Salt

2 ounces (60 g) daikon, peeled, cut into matchsticks (about ½ cup)

½ cup (80 g) Marinated Mushrooms (page 31), thinly sliced

2 sheets Marinated Fried Tofu (page 34), thinly sliced

14 oz (400 g) Marinated Konnyaku (see recipe opposite page), or your favorite noodle, such as soba, udon, or angel hair pasta, slightly undercooked and marinated per the konnyaku instructions (replacing the "blanched konnyaku" with the noodles)

5-COLOR SALAD DRESSING

2 tablespoons rice wine vinegar

1 tablespoon sugar

½ teaspoon prepared hot mustard (Japanese, Chinese or Colman's)

½ teaspoon salt

1. Toss the cucumber with salt (about 1 heaping teaspoon) in a small bowl until evenly coated. Set aside.

2. Meanwhile, bring a pan of salted water to a boil. Add the daikon and blanch for 1 minute. (Blanching the daikon in salted water removes some of its bitterness.) Drain, and immediately place in ice water. When cooled, drain and roll in paper towel to dry.

3. To make the 5-Color Salad Dressing, whisk together the ingredients in a small bowl. Set aside.

4. Rinse off the cucumbers, drain, and then gently squeeze dry.

5. Combine the cucumber, blanched daikon, Marinated Mushrooms, Marinated Fried Tofu and Marinated Konnyaku in a serving bowl. Pour the 5-Color Salad Dressing over and toss.

Cooking Tip *If you're making a fresh batch of Marinated Mushrooms for this recipe, reserve ¼ cup (65 ml) of the soaking liquid for the Marinated Konnyaku. Though the konnyaku can be marinated in water, it will have a much richer flavor if marinated in the reserved mushroom water.*

Marinated Konnyaku

One of the most distinctive ingredients in this salad is *konnyaku*, a gelatinous product made from a yam/potato plant known by the very same name. Konnyaku comes in either blocklike form or long noodlelike strands known as *shirataki*, which are called for in this recipe. I must say, there is something mysterious about konnyaku. And its English names—"elephant foot" and "devil's tongue"—provide no further clarification. Konnyaku itself has very little taste, though it will absorb the flavors of the dish it's cooked in. Konnyaku is often included in recipes for its chewy texture.

MAKES 14 OZ (400 G)

3 tablespoons soy sauce
2 tablespoons sugar
1 teaspoon instant dashi powder
¼ cup (65ml) reserved mushroom water (from Marinated Mushrooms recipe, page 31) or water
One 14-oz (400-g) package shirataki konnyaku, roughly cut to your preferred "noodle" length and blanched

Bring the soy sauce, sugar, instant dashi powder and water to a boil in a small saucepan. Add the blanched konnyaku and simmer over medium-low heat for 10 minutes, or until the sauce has been absorbed. Drain off any excess liquid.

White Radish Salad

The first time I lived in Japan my mom came to visit me. One night, I took her to Hiromi's restaurant, Kyosaka, and we ordered this salad. The next time I went to Japan, my mom told me to not bother coming home if I didn't bring this recipe with me.

The ingredient that gives this salad its irresistible flavor is *karashimentaiko*, spicy salted cod roe. If unable to find the spicy version and using salted cod roe (*mentaiko*) instead, mix one teaspoon of Sriracha, or other chili sauce, in with the mayonnaise. Note that although you can use any brand of mayonnaise, this recipe especially benefits from the extra tangy Japanese variety—available at Asian markets and large grocery stores.

SERVES 4

1 spicy salted cod roe (karashimentaiko) (about 1½ oz/40 g)

1 whole daikon (about 1 lb/500 g), washed and ends trimmed

½ cup (100 g) mayonnaise

2 tablespoons saké

Red leaf lettuce leaves, rinsed and patted dry

Slivered nori, for garnish (optional)

1. To prepare the spicy salted cod roe, follow the illustrated steps in "Preparing Roe," right.

2. Using a vegetable peeler, peel off and discard the tough outer skin of the daikon. Then shave long ribbons along the length of the daikon with a vegetable peeler. Pat the ribbons dry with paper towels.

3. Whisk together the mayonnaise, roe, and saké in a small bowl until combined. Set aside.

4. To serve, in a large bowl, toss together the daikon ribbons and ¼ cup (50 g) of the mayonnaise dressing, or to taste. (You will most likely have additional dressing left over. Save for another use or for second helpings.) Alternately, you can serve the dressing on the side, allowing each person to dress their own salad.

5. Line four serving bowls with lettuce leaves. Divide the daikon among the bowls, mounding the portions in the middle of each bowl. Garnish with the slivered nori, if desired. Serve with the dressing on the side if you have not already dressed the daikon.

Cooking Tip *You can purchase nori already slivered. If unavailable, buy whatever size nori sheets you are able to find, and then cut with kitchen shears into long, thin strips (approximately 2 x ¼-inch/5 cm x 6-mm)—or whatever size strips you have the patience to trim the nori down to.*

Preparing Roe

1. Slice the karashimentaiko *in half lengthwise to slit open the thin outer lining.*

2. You may use a spoon to gently scrape the roe out of the thin lining, as shown in the photograph; or, use your fingers to gently squeeze out the roe. Discard the lining.

White Radish Salad

Garlic Chive Pancakes

This is the first recipe Reiko taught me. Having gone into the Obuse Guide Center café for a pot of morning tea, I sat at a table making friendly conversation with the owner, who then introduced me to Reiko, the café's chef. Hearing of my interest in Japanese food, Reiko whisked me off to her garden out back to pick fresh *nira* (garlic chives) and then into her kitchen to prepare these popular homestyle pancakes. Everyone in the café was thankful for my inquisitiveness since Reiko generously passed around samples to all the hungry customers listening in.

MAKES APPROXIMATELY 12 SMALL PANCAKES OR 1 LARGE PANCAKE

1 recipe Sanbaizu Sauce (omit garlic) (page 134), for dipping
2 eggs
1 tablespoon miso
¼ cup (36 g) all-purpose flour
⅓ cup (24 g) diced garlic chives (or ½ cup/35 g diced regular chives)
Oil, for frying

1. Make the Sanbaizu Sauce, but omit the garlic. Set aside.
2. To make the batter, whisk together the eggs and miso in a small bowl until combined. Whisk in the flour until smooth, and then stir in the chives.
3. Heat 1 teaspoon of oil in a skillet over low heat. When hot, pour 2 teaspoons of batter per pancake into the skillet and cook until lightly browned and cooked through, about 2 to 3 minutes per side. The pancakes are ready to flip when tiny bubbles on the top surface pop and don't fill in.
4. Continue as directed above until all the batter has been used up, adding more oil to grease the skillet as needed.
5. Serve immediately while warm. Use the Sanbaizu Sauce for dipping.

Serving Tip *The batter can be formed into individual pancakes or one large party size pancake, which is then sliced like a pie before serving.*

CHAPTER 2

Soups

We're all familiar with miso soup, and it *is* wonderfully delicious. But Japan is full of soups beyond the iconic miso variety—noodle soups, creamy soups, dumpling soups . . . the list goes on. Fish Stock (*Dashi*), the base of many of these recipes, is made from three simple ingredients: water, *konbu* (a variety of kelp) and *katsuobushi* (dried bonito fish flakes), which imparts a hint of smoky flavor. If you're a vegetarian, simply substitute with one of the vegetarian options such as the delicate Vegetarian Stock or the earthy Shiitake Mushroom Stock (pages 26 and 27).

There are two main types of vegetarian soup in Japan: *Kenchinjiru* (*jiru* meaning "soup") and *umpinjiru*. Umpinjiru is a Chinese-style, thick, chowderlike soup usually made with a slurry of cornstarch mixed with cold dashi or water. Typically, umpinjiru contains no tofu. Kenchinjiru, on the other hand, has a clear broth full of colorful root and tuber vegetables as well as some sort of tofu, most commonly *momen* (regular) or *abura-age* (fried).

A tip for keeping soup warmer, longer: Before serving, heat the soup bowls by either placing them in a warm oven, or fill them with hot water (if serving a noodle soup, use the water the noodles were boiled in) and let sit for a minute or two before draining and ladling in the warm soup.

Miso Soup with Baby Clams

The best part about making miso soup is that there are few rules. Once you get the hang of making the base—slowing blending miso into warm *dashi*—the type of miso used and the variety of additional ingredients is endless.

A great technique to practice is *awase miso*—the blending together of different types of miso, for example a light and a dark, to provide a richer, more complex flavor.

When making miso soup, the general rule is one tablespoon of miso per one cup (250 ml) of stock, allowing for freedom to adjust for personal preference. Just don't let the stock boil once the miso has been added—it will destroy the miso's delicate flavor and texture.

Adding Miso to Soup

• When adding miso to soup broth, it's important to do so slowly to allow it to evenly incorporate. In Japan, I was taught to do this by placing the miso on a flat strainer-spoon, and then gently massaging the miso into the liquid (see the above photograph).

• Another method, which I find easier, is to ladle some broth into a small bowl. Whisk in the miso until dissolved, and then slowing pour this mixture back into the stockpot, stirring to combine.

• Note that miso doesn't fully dissolve into broth, so it's quick to separate and settle at the bottom of serving bowls. That's okay. Just give the broth a quick swirl with your chopsticks or spoon between sips.

SERVES 4

4 cups (1 liter) Fish Stock (page 26)

1 lb (500 g) hard-shelled clams of your choice (about 20 Manila clams, 10 littlenecks or 8 cherrystones), prepared (see tips on this page)

4 tablespoons miso

2 tablespoons dried wakame, hydrated and cut into smaller pieces

1 package (3½ oz/100 g) fresh enoki mushrooms, ends trimmed and separated

1. Bring the Fish Stock to a simmer in a medium pot over medium-high heat. Reduce the heat to low, add the clams and cover. Cook just until the clams open, about 3 minutes. Remove the open clams with a slotted spoon. If any of the clams did not open, return the lid and continue cooking 1 to 2 minutes more. Remove the additional opened clams and set aside with the other open clams, discarding any that did not open. If you're worried that silt was released during cooking, strain the broth through a coffee filter or cheesecloth-lined fine-mesh sieve. Return the broth to the pot and heat on low.

2. Whisk the miso into the broth following the instructions in the sidebar at left.

3. To serve, divide the cooked clams, *wakame* and enoki among the four bowls. Pour the stock over and serve warm.

Tips for Storing and Preparing Hard-shelled Clams

• *Plan on 2 to 5 clams per serving, depending on the size of the clams you use.*

• *Store the clams in the refrigerator until ready to use, being sure to open the plastic bag the clams were sold in; otherwise, they will suffocate. Stored properly, the clams should last up to 5 days in the refrigerator.*

• *Clams should not be soaked in fresh water. They will drown. If the clams are sitting in a bag of ice, be sure to poke holes in the bottom for the water to drain off as the ice melts.*

• *Hard-shell clams are usually fully closed when purchased. (If open, gently squeeze down on the shell. If the clam doesn't close on its own within 1 minute, discard.)*

• *Since these hard-shell clams are already closed, they should be, in theory, silt-free. So there is no need to soak them in salt water before use (a common step in the preparation of clams). To prepare, simply rinse well under cold water, or scrub the outside of the shells if especially dirty.*

• *When cooking, all of the clams may not open at the same time. This is why it's best to check on the clams in stages—first after three minutes of cooking, and then again after another minute or two.*

Soy Sauce Soup With Rice Crackers Nambu Senbei Jiru

I had planned for only a short visit to Aomori. In the course of the prior evening's conversation, I learned that the area was a veritable mecca of *onsen* (hot springs), and there was no way I was going to pass up sampling some of them. I had to stay another night!

After a long day of hiking through snowy mountains from one onsen to the next—including my first ever dip into a mixed-gender bath (fortunately, the steam was thick enough; the water milky enough)—I was greeted at the dinner table by a warm bowl of this filling soup.

Nambu Senbei Jiru is another version of the economical soy sauce dumpling soup (see page 64), but in this case, plain *nambu senbei* crackers are used for the dumplings. "Nambu" is in reference to an old prefectural name, just as Tokyo used to be called Edo. Rumor has it that when samurai went off to war, they would nourish themselves with these crackers before going into battle. They'd make a simple dough of flour and water that was then pressed into their metal helmets, thrown into the fire and "baked." Plain or sesame is the traditional flavor, but today you can find them flavored with almost anything, including chocolate.

SERVES 6

1 leek, green top reserved

8 cups (2 liters) chicken broth

10 oz (300 g) daikon, peeled, cut into ¼-in (6-mm)-thick half moons (2 cups)

2 large carrots, peeled, cut into ¼-in (6-mm)-thick half moons (2 cups)

3 tablespoons saké

2 tablespoons soy sauce

1 teaspoon salt, or to taste

7 oz (200 g) fresh mushrooms, assorted

Rice crackers (senbei), broken into large pieces

1. To clean the leek, slice it in half lengthwise and then run water between each of its layers. Shake dry. Cut off the green top portion, tie each half together with kitchen twine, and set aside. (If you don't have kitchen twine, ignore this step; the twine simply holds the green tops together while simmering.) Thinly slice the remaining white portion of the leek. Set aside for garnish.

2. Bring the chicken broth to a simmer in a large stockpot.

3. Add the daikon, carrot and green leek tops and simmer for 10 minutes, or until the vegetables are just starting to soften.

4. Add the saké, soy sauce and salt. Stir to combine.

5. Add the mushrooms and simmer until the vegetables are tender, about 5 minutes more. (Quarter any large mushrooms before adding.)

6. Garnish with the reserved sliced leek whites and rice crackers.

Cooking Tips *The broth of this soup is traditionally made by simmering tori gara (chicken carcass) in water for 30 minutes, and then straining it. For convenience, I use pre-made chicken broth.*

Depending on the area in which it's being made, chicken, pork, or fish is added to the soup. Sweet potato, for example, is included in the southern part of Japan, where it grows in abundance. You can customize the soup as you like, but be aware that adding meat will make the soup heavier and more oily.

While it's common to add the rice crackers directly to the soup, I much prefer to dunk them one at a time, just until they start to absorb the broth, and then enjoy.

A Note About Dumplings

This style of soy sauce soup is typically served with dumplings rather than crackers. Depending on the region of Japan, the dumplings can go by different names. In Tono, the dumplings are referred to as hittsumi, *in Obuse as* suiton, *and in Oita prefecture as* dango, *where the dumpling dough is stretched into long noodles. But whatever the name, their origin is the same: The flour dumplings are a product of Japan's wartime poverty. With rice too expensive—or unavailable—the dumplings, made simply from flour and water, became the common fare.*

The texture is purely personal preference. When making the dumplings, take the measurements provided loosely: Some people prefer the dough to be softer (which requires using more water); a tougher dough would use less water. The ear lobe is a common medium used in Japan to describe a dough's texture—whether a recipe calls for "softer than," "the same as," or "harder than," the ear lobe is almost always the standard setting.

While Reiko just drops her dumplings directly into the broth to cook, this method only works for immediate eating—the dumplings don't keep well in the liquid, turning unappetizingly mushy. The technique used in the Pork Soup with Dumplings recipe (page 64)—cooking the dumplings separately and then adding to each individual serving—includes an extra step, but also keeps the dumplings fresher longer. With this method, you can save leftovers in a separate container, and then add to the re-heated soup just before serving.

2 tablespoons oil

2½ oz (75 g) daikon, peeled and sliced in ¼-in (6-mm)-thick half moons (about ½ cup)

½ cup (45 g) scrubbed and shaved burdock (see "Shaving Vegetables," page 15) (optional)

½ cup (30 g) thinly sliced fresh mushrooms, such as eringi, shimeji, or shiitake

1 small carrot, peeled and sliced in ¼-in (6-mm) thick half moons (about ⅓ cup)

One 3 x 5-in (7.5 x 12.75-cm) sheet fried tofu (abura-age), rolled in paper towel to remove excess oil and thinly sliced

⅓ lb (150 g) boneless pork chops, thinly sliced and lightly seasoned with salt and pepper

4 cups (1 liter) Fish Stock (page 26)

2 tablespoons miso

1 Welsh onion or 1 small leek (about 8 in/20 cm long), thinly sliced, or more to taste

1. Add the oil to a stockpot over medium-high heat and sauté the daikon, burdock, mushrooms, carrot and fried tofu sheet until they start to soften, about 3 minutes. Add the pork and sauté 1 minute more. Pour in the Fish Stock and, over medium-high heat, bring just to a boil. The pork should now be cooked (it will be white with just a slight hint of pink in the middle when cut in half). If not, lower the heat to medium-low and simmer until cooked through. (Watch the pork carefully as it is quick to overcook, turning tough and chewy.)

2. Whisk the miso into the soup following the steps in "Adding Miso to Soup" on page 55.

3. Distribute the sliced onion or leek among four serving bowls. Top with the soup and serve.

Pork and Leek Miso Soup
Tonjiru

*T*on means "pork" in Japanese, and according to Hitomi, without pork and leeks on hand, don't even bother making this soup—they're the two essential ingredients that, for her, make it worth eating.

Tonjiru is especially popular at any outdoor event in winter—like school fieldtrips, where at least one mom is guaranteed to bring this soup: it's healthy and helps keep the body warm.

Fava Bean Soup
Nokorimono Soramamejiru

Still tired from a late evening at the restaurant the night before, Hiromi quickly whipped up this creamy soup for lunch one day—taking advantage of whatever ingredients she happened to have on hand (*nokorimono* means "leftovers" in Japanese). The most memorable part of the meal, as we silently dined in her traditionally decorated home, was the techno music thumping away in the background. Hiromi's son had sent her the CD, and she had anxiously turned it on for us to enjoy—an attempt to entertain the foreigner sitting across from her as well as a tribute to her globe-trotting son, presently kidnapped by the lures of New York City.

Being the avid chef that she is, Hiromi prepared this soup using the many seasonal ingredients with which her refrigerator is continually stocked—fava beans among them. In the spirit of Hiromi's kitchen, I like to use fresh fava beans whenever I can find them. But I'm not going to deny that it's time-consuming to work with the beans. Their flavor is well worth the two-step process required, though. If pressed for time, prepared (shucked and hulled) fava beans are available in the frozen-foods section of larger grocery stores and Asian markets. And if fresh or frozen prepared fava beans are unavailable, the more widely available *edamame* (soybeans) may be substituted.

SERVES 4

- 1½ lbs (750 g) fresh fava beans (still in the pod) or 1½ cups prepared frozen fava beans (150 g) or frozen shelled edamame (255 g)
- 1 lb (500 g) Yukon gold potatoes, peeled and cut into large chunks
- 3 cups (750 ml) whole milk, divided
- 1 cup (250 ml) water
- 1 chicken bouillon cube
- Salt and fresh cracked white pepper, to taste
- 4 dollops lightly salted whipped cream, for garnish (optional)

1. To shuck fresh fava beans, open the pods by pulling the little string along the length of the pod. Once "unzipped", you can remove the beans inside. You should have 1½ cups (150 g) shucked fava beans.

2. Bring a small stockpot of water to a boil. Blanch the shucked fava beans for 1 minute. Immediately drain and place in a bowl of ice water to prevent overcooking. When the beans are cool-to-the-touch, drain. To hull the beans, remove the tough outer membrane of the bean by first peeling off a corner of the skin, and then "popping," or pushing, the bean out. Set the hulled beans aside.

3. Bring a medium stockpot of lightly salted water to a boil. Add the potatoes and boil until fork tender, about 15 to 20 minutes. Drain, and then immediately mash the hot potatoes with the back of a fork until smooth. Measure out 2 cups (225 g) of the mashed potatoes, reserving any extra for another use. Set aside.

4. Combine the prepared beans (reserving about a dozen for garnish) and 2 cups (500 ml) milk in a blender and puree until smooth. Add the 2 cups (225 g) of mashed potatoes and continue to blend until smooth and velvety.

5. Pour the slurry into a large saucepan. Add the remaining 1 cup (250 ml) milk, water and bouillon cube and, whisking occasionally, heat on medium heat for 10 minutes, or until warmed through and the bouillon has dissolved. Season with the salt and pepper.

6. Divide the soup among four bowls and garnish each with a few of the reserved fava beans. For a sophisticated garnish, add a dollop of whipped cream, if desired. This soup tastes best if enjoyed the same day it is made.

Cooking Tips *To save time and streamline the soup-making process, the fava beans and potatoes can be prepared a day ahead. To keep the soup as frothy as possible, blend and heat through just before serving. The longer the time lapse between the two, the flatter the soup will appear. Whisking the soup while heating will also help to maintain its velvety texture. If you don't have a blender, don't substitute with a food processor. The potatoes will take on a gluelike consistency.*

BURDOCK SOUP
GOBO JIRU

An Enjoyable Evening

I arrived late at night, the rural bus dropping me off along the dark, desolate highway; the only light illuminating the hostel's welcoming front door. Too late for dinner, I joined Hideo, the hostel owner, and his only other guest for teatime in the common room. With Hideo acting as the interpreter for my broken Japanese and the other guest's broken English, the three of us managed to have a very enjoyable evening.

The other guest had recently retired from his "salary man" position after a close friend died from a heart attack caused by overworking. Not wanting to meet the same fate, he set off on his bicycle for a three-year solo tour of Japan, leaving his wife and son at home.

He labeled himself an Edo-ko. (Edo being the old name for Tokyo.) An Edo-ko, he explained, is like a classic New Yorker. People don't tend to leave the city, travel outside their daily routine. And with Japan being a small country, the scale of "your world" is much smaller. While driving six hours in the United States is considered no big deal, the distance is considered outrageous in Japan. So, after living under this constricted mentality for years, he's now making up for lost time.

And so we continued to talk, warming ourselves with freshly steeped rosehip tea—the pink rosebuds still floating in the glass teapot, and snacking on kori mochi (freeze-dried rice crackers), which a friend of Hideo's had made and so generously shared with him.

Vitamin-rich burdock is as much of a grocery staple in Japan as apples are in the United States, and it was at another of Hiromi's popular cooking classes that I was first introduced to this fantastic soup. Although burdock may not be the most attractive of the root vegetables, what this soup lacks in appearance (an uninspiring pale brown color), it quickly makes up for in flavor!

If the stock I'm using isn't particularly full-bodied, I sometimes add a bouillon cube to boost its flavor. If you're using homemade chicken stock, though, you probably won't need to use this trick.

SERVES 6

1 tablespoon butter
1 tablespoon oil
1 cup (150 g) diced onion
2 cups (260 g) diced burdock
1 cup (180 g) peeled and diced Yukon gold potato
1 teaspoon salt
2 ½ cups (625 ml) chicken stock
1 chicken bouillon cube (optional)
1²/₃ cups (400 ml) milk
Toasted black and white sesame seeds (see "Toasting Sesame Seeds," page 16)

1. Add the butter and oil to a large stockpot over medium-high heat. Add the onions and sauté until they start to turn transparent, about 5 minutes. Add the burdock, potatoes and salt and continue sautéing 5 minutes more, or until the vegetables just start to brown. Pour in the stock and bring to a boil. Lower the heat and simmer, uncovered, until the potatoes are fork-tender, about 15 minutes. Taste and if you feel the soup's flavor is a little thin, add the bouillon cube and stir until dissolved.

2. Carefully pour the hot soup into a blender and puree until smooth. Over medium-low heat, return the soup to the stockpot, add the milk and, stirring occasionally, heat through.

3. Garnish with toasted sesame seeds before serving.

Cooking Tips *There is no need to peel the burdock, just trim off the ends and use a vegetable brush to scrub clean. As you're preparing the burdock, place the cleaned pieces in a bowl of acidulated water (water with a small amount of lemon juice or vinegar added) to keep it from discoloring. It's important to dice both the burdock and potato to similar size to ensure even cooking.*

Get-Well-Soon Udon Soup
Kenchin Udon

This is Hitomi's cure-all soup and the one she made for Hiromi, her aunt and culinary mentor, when she was too sick to get out of bed, let alone cook for herself. And when my husband had a nagging winter cold that wouldn't go away, I made him this soup. It was the only food he had the appetite to eat—two full bowls of!

SERVES 6

4 oz (125 g) dried udon noodles

6 cups (1.5 liters) Fish Stock (page 26)

4 boneless, skinless chicken thighs (about 1 lb/500 g), cut into 1-in (2.5-cm) pieces

4 oz (125 g) daikon, peeled and sliced into half moons (about 1 cup)

1 medium carrot, peeled and sliced into half moons (about 1 cup)

1 cup (60 g) thinly sliced fresh mushrooms, such as eringi or shiitake

One 3 x 5-in (7.5 x 12.75-cm) sheet fried tofu (abura-age), rolled in paper towel to remove excess oil and thinly sliced

One 4¾-oz (136-g) block firm tofu, pressed dry and cubed

1 cup (80 g) thinly sliced leek, or more to taste

2 tablespoons saké

1 tablespoon salt

1 tablespoon soy sauce

1. Bring a pot of water to a boil. Cook the *udon* according to package instructions (generally about 8 to 10 minutes). Drain, rinse, and drain again. Set aside.

2. Meanwhile, bring the Fish Stock just to a boil in a large saucepan. Reduce the heat to medium, add the chicken and simmer for 5 minutes, or until cooked through. Reduce the heat to low. Add the daikon, carrot, mushrooms, sliced fried tofu sheet, firm tofu and leek and simmer 10 minutes more, or until the vegetables are tender.

3. Stir in the salt, saké and soy sauce.

4. Return the cooked udon to the pot, heat through and serve warm.

Cooking Tip *Although the presence of soy sauce does add some flavor, its purpose in this recipe is to add color—salt is already used as a main seasoning agent, and with soy sauce's naturally high sodium content, you want to be careful not to go overboard.*

Mixed Tofu Soup Dofujiru

In addition to the long, late hours her restaurant demands, Hiromi also teaches cooking classes on Tuesdays, her one day off each week. This recipe is one of my favorites from the Tofu Cooking Class I was fortunate enough to assist with.

This recipe for *Dofujiru* gives new meaning to soy. Soy's three derivatives—*tofu* (soy bean curd), *tonyu* (soy milk), and *yuba* (soy milk skin)—are all blended together with roasted eggplant. The exquisite pairing of flavors is so perfect you'll wonder why you never thought of it yourself.

SERVES 6

1 sheet yuba (soy milk skin), about 20 x 10 in (50 x 25 cm)

3 Japanese eggplants

½ onion, sliced thinly

½ Yukon gold potato, peeled and sliced thinly

2 tablespoons butter or oil

½ block soft tofu (about 8 oz/250 g), cubed

4 cups (1 liter) plain, unsweetened soy milk, divided

6 tablespoons miso, preferably white

Garlic chives (nira) or chives, for garnish

1. If using dried yuba, soak the yuba in a bowl of hot water while preparing the other ingredients, about 5 minutes, or until softened. Drain. Cut the yuba into bite-sized squares.

2. Pierce the eggplants with a fork or skewer, place on an ungreased sheet pan and broil until very soft, about 15 minutes. (Alternatively, you can bake the eggplants at 350°F/175 C° for about an hour.) When cool-to-the-touch, peel the eggplants, squeeze out any excess moisture, and cut into bite-size pieces. Set aside.

3. Cook the onions and potatoes in butter in a medium skillet over medium heat until tender, about 10 minutes. Place the cooked vegetables in a medium bowl and pour in 2 cups (500 ml) of the soy milk. Stir to combine.

4. Place the vegetable and soy milk mixture in a blender along with the tofu and miso. Blend until smooth.

5. Place the contents of the blender plus the remaining soy milk in a large pot. Heat over medium-low heat to warm through.

6. To serve, divide the eggplant and softened yuba among each of the six bowls. Ladle in the soup and garnish with the chives.

Cooking Tip *As noted in* A Dictionary of Japanese Food *by Richard Hosking, yuba, the skin formed when soy milk is heated, is the richest source of protein known (over 52 percent)! It is also called "bean curd sheets" or "bean curd skins" and has a very chewy texture. Although fresh is preferred, it is much more readily available in its dried state. If working with dried yuba, reconstitute before use.*

Pork Soup with Dumplings Nambu Hitssumi

Although known for its folklore and the ever-famous Kappa "river monster," I, instead, came to Tono for the food. And from the moment I arrived I tried to get myself invited into the kitchen of the youth hostel where I was staying. Modest, and a little confused by my intentions—I doubt any previous guest had ever expressed interest in her world behind the curtain—I finally convinced Ms. Konkawa, the hostel manager, to allow me to keep her company while she prepared the evening meal.

That night, Nambu Hitssumi was on the menu. The concept of the soup is found all over Japan. Tono personalizes the dish by first stretching the dumpling dough before adding it to the soup. The result is a flat, paper-, or orecchiette pastalike dumpling. (When I ate the soup with Reiko in Obuse, she shaped her dumplings into the more traditional ball form, dropping them directly into the soup to cook. See "A Note About Dumplings," page 56).

With all the guests huddled around the communal tables, and after the introduction of the evening's meal concluded with an "*itadakimasu*" ("bon appétit") in unison, every camera, cell phone, and any other electronic device with photographic capabilities was capturing the meal in which they were about to indulge. And knowing I helped in its preparation, all the Japanese guests were asking me, the American(!), to better explain the soup and dumplings they were so unfamiliar with and held in such high esteem.

Here is what I learned from Ms. Konkawa: The meat is flexible—even optional. Ms. Konkawa uses pork because it's what her husband prefers, but chicken works just as well. Or, for a vegetarian option, omit the meat altogether. For a hint of sweetness, add a few dashes of mirin when adding the soy sauce to the soup. For a paler broth, use *usukuchi shoyu* (light-colored soy sauce). And the best tip of all: making the dumplings goes much faster if you can have one person scooping out the cooked dumplings while the other continues to shape them.

SERVES 6

DUMPLINGS
1¼ cups plus 2 tablespoons (200 g) all-purpose flour
½ cup (125 ml) water

SOUP
1 tablespoon oil
1 lb (500 g) boneless pork chops, thinly sliced and lightly seasoned with salt and pepper
1 cup (100 g) shaved or chopped carrot (about 1 whole)
½ lb (250 g) daikon, peeled and sliced into ¼-in (6-mm)-thick half moons (about 1 cup)
One 3½-oz (100-g) package fresh enoki mushrooms, ends trimmed and separated
3 oz (80 g) fresh shimeji mushrooms, cleaned and trimmed (about 1 cup)
3 oz (80 g) fresh maitake mushrooms, cleaned and trimmed (about 1 cup)
8 cups (2 liters) water
¼ cup (65 ml) soy sauce
1 teaspoon salt
2 tablespoons saké
2 teaspoons instant dashi powder
Mitsuba (Japanese Wild Chervil), stemmed and coarsely chopped, for garnish (substitute mizuna, arugula, or watercress)
Shichimi togarashi or ground red pepper (cayenne), to taste (optional)

Cooking Tips *If unable to find the mushroom varieties specified, use equal amounts of what's available, such as shiitake or crimini.*

In this recipe, shaved carrots are called for (see "Shaving Vegetables," page 15). If eating the soup with chopsticks, this cut works just fine. But if using a spoon, you may want to consider cutting the carrots into smaller chunks that are easier to scoop up.

1. To make the dough for the Dumplings, mix together the flour and water in a small bowl. When the dough starts to hold its shape, turn out onto a lightly floured surface and knead until smooth, about 5 minutes. Return the dough to the bowl (it's best if cleaned out first), cover with plastic wrap, and let the dough rest, about 30 minutes.

2. To make the Dumplings, follow the illustrated steps on the opposite page.

3. To make the Soup, add the oil to a large stockpot over medium-high heat. Add the pork and sauté until browned, 1 to 2 minutes. Transfer to a plate with a slotted spoon.

4. Add the carrot and daikon to the stockpot and sauté, stirring constantly, for 2 minutes, or until just starting to brown. Add the mushrooms and sauté until slightly wilted, about 1 minute.

5. Add the water and bring to a simmer. Then add the soy sauce, salt, saké and instant dashi powder. Add the pork and continue to simmer for about 5 minutes, being careful not to overcook the pork.

6. To serve, fill individual bowls with the cooked dumplings and chopped *mitsuba*. Top with the Soup. Or, for family-style dining, put the soup pot on the table and let people help themselves. Sprinkle on some *shichimi togarashi*, if desired.

1. Bring a large pot of water to a boil to cook the dumplings.

2. Gently knead the dumpling dough and place on a lightly floured surface. Have a large bowl of ice water nearby.

3. With lightly floured hands, break off a quarter-size piece of dough. Roll it between your hands to form a ball, and then flatten and stretch from its four "corners" to form a small, thin square.

4. Drop the dumpling into the boiling water. When it floats to the top (after about 45 seconds), use a slotted spoon to transfer it to the ice water. Repeat with the remaining dough. Remove the cooked dumplings from the ice water, rinse, and set aside. (It is okay to boil the dumplings in batches).

Udon Soup with Chicken Meatballs
Tori Gara Udon

From the moment we arrived at Takeko's remote A-frame mountain retreat in Nagano prefecture, her daughter Yukari was put to work preparing the chicken meatballs for this delicious soup. The meatballs were made from a frozen chicken carcass. And all activities performed that morning were underscored by the continual metronome-like banging of Yukari, out on the back porch, sledge hammer in hand, rhythmically pounding away on the carcass, which had been placed inside a pillow case. The bones breaking and crunching, breaking and crunching, until the pulverized carcass miraculously turned tender—an extraordinarily laborious task I'd never before considered. (Fortunately, the recipe that follows calls for ground chicken, instead.) It seems this frugal technique was actually an extremely hospitable gesture. As I was later informed, chicken was considered a delicacy by the war-affected generation. Thus, it was only when special guests were invited to dine that a chicken was butchered and a feast had. For such an occasion, Yukari was unfortunately estranged from the social goings-on of the morning.

SERVES 6

4 oz (125 g) dried udon noodles

MEATBALLS
½ lb (500 g) ground chicken
1 teaspoon salt
¾ teaspoon shichimi togarashi or ¼ teaspoon ground red pepper (cayenne), or to taste

SOUP
8 cups (2 liters) water
1 cup (100 g) shaved burdock (about 1 whole) (optional)
1 cup (60 g) sliced fresh mushrooms, preferably eringi or shiitake
One 3 x 5-in (7.5 x 12.75-cm) sheet fried tofu (abura-age), rolled in paper towel to remove excess oil, thinly sliced
½ cup (40 g) thinly sliced leek
¼ cup (65 ml) soy sauce

1. Bring a pot of water to a boil. Cook the *udon* according to packaged instructions (about 8 to 10 minutes). Drain, rinse, and drain again. Set aside.

2. To make the Meatballs, combine the ingredients in a small bowl. With damp hands, form 1 teaspoon of the mixture into a ball. Repeat with remaining mixture; you should have about 18 Meatballs.

3. To make the Soup, bring the water to a boil in the same pot used to boil the udon. Add the burdock, if using, and the mushrooms and fried tofu. Reduce the heat to medium and simmer 5 minutes. Add the Meatballs, cover, reduce the heat to low and cook 5 minutes more, or until the Meatballs are cooked through. Add the leek, soy sauce and cooked udon. Cook 1 minute more to heat through.

Cooking Tips *Unless you use a monstrous pot, the water has a tendency to boil over as the udon cooks. To prevent this from happening, do as Takeko does: Add a small amount of cold water to the pot as it gets restless.*

Unlike Italian pastas, udon noodles need to be rinsed after cooking or they'll be too slimy.

Since the noodles are to be added to the hot soup before serving, cook them until they are slightly underdone. They will continue to soften in the warm broth.

Somen Noodle Miso Soup
Somenjiru

T his soup continues to amaze me. It's made from just three ingredients (+ water). The broth is so incredibly light and delicate, possessing such understated perfection. The only thing you're left wanting is another refill.

I was taught this recipe on the southern "island" of Shikoku, where *iriko dashi*, stock made with dried sardines (*niboshi*), is the norm—as opposed to the more common dashi made from dried bonito fish flakes (*katsuobushi*) (page 26). Iriko dashi has a much more robust flavor and is often used to make miso soup, as this recipe demonstrates.

To prevent the stock from turning bitter, you will need to remove the head and belly cavity from the dried sardines. This process is similar to deveining a shrimp but easier since the fish are dried and the parts break right off. At first, you might not know where the "belly cavity" is, but once you start the process, you will quickly be able to infer. Behind the head and under the backbone there will be a clump of dried black matter. This is what you will want to remove along with the head. Preparing dried sardines may seem gross, tedious, and worth avoiding altogether, but I assure you, it is quick, easy, and painless. Take note that the size (length and/or weight) of dried sardines can vary greatly. Because of the large variation, it's best to go by the weight measurements below.

SERVES 4

¾ oz (20 g) dried sardines (about 8 large or 80 small), prepared (see instructions on opposite page)

4 cups (1 liter) water or Vegetarian Stock (page 27)

3 oz (85 g) dried somen noodles (1 bunch)

4 tablespoons miso

2 green onions (scallions), thinly sliced, green part only, for garnish

1. To make the dried sardine stock (iriko dashi), soak the prepared sardines in a medium pot in the water or Vegetarian Stock at room temperature for 30 minutes.

2. Meanwhile, bring a pot of water to a boil. Cook the *somen* according to packaged instructions (about 2 to 3 minutes). Drain, rinse, and drain again. Set aside.

3. When the sardines are finished soaking, bring the water or stock they are soaking in to a boil. Then, reduce the heat and simmer for 5 minutes. Strain the stock through a cheesecloth, coffee filter or fine-mesh sieve. Discard the sardines.

4. Return the strained stock to the pot and heat over a low flame. Do not let boil.

5. Whisk the miso into the soup following the instructions in "Adding Miso to Soup" on page 55.

6. To serve, divide the cooked somen noodles among four bowls. Pour the stock over and garnish with the sliced green onions. Serve immediately.

Special Equipment *Cheesecloth, coffee filter or fine-mesh sieve*

Preparing Sardines

1. To remove the head, hold the tail with one hand, and with the thumb and index finger of your other hand, pinch just below the head and pull up and backward to break it off. Some of the belly cavity may come off with the head.

2. To remove the belly cavity, hold the tail with one hand and pull the belly cavity out. The "belly cavity" is the dried black matter—a thick black "vein"—located behind the head and under the backbone. Discard the head and belly cavity but be sure to keep the skeleton and remaining meaty parts for the stock!

CHAPTER 3

Rice and Noodles

Udon, soba, somen, ramen, chuka soba, cold noodles, fried noodles, noodle soups … who knew there were so many varieties?!

As much as rice is part of the Japanese diet, so too are noodles.

In a marked difference from the preparation of Italian pastas, Japanese noodles are always rinsed under cold water after boiling. The reason for this step will be obvious to anyone who omits it—without rinsing, the noodles take on an unappetizingly slimy texture.

When it comes to rice, there are at least two methods for making it: *Taki-kome,* in which the rice is cooked with some liquid other than water, like tea or *dashi*; and *maze-gohan,* in which plain white rice is tossed with additional ingredients (see, for example, the recipe for Sushi Rice with Toppings, page 81).

Many of the rice dishes included in this chapter are not meals unto themselves but rather a delicious variation on the traditional staple. While plain white rice is always welcome, try mixing things up a bit by serving one of these "flavored" rice dishes, instead.

Almond Rice Onigiri

Essentially nothing more than a formed rice ball wrapped in a sheet of nori, *Onigiri* is the peanut butter and jelly of Japanese cuisine—a staple in every child's and salary man's lunch box, and a given at any *hanami* (cherry blossom viewing picnic). No road trip or long-distance train ride would be complete without first stopping at the local *konbini* (convenience store) where Onigiri is sold ingeniously packaged—the wrapper separating the rice from the crisp seaweed, preventing the rice from prematurely turning the nori soggy.

The varieties of Onigiri are endless: plain white rice stuffed with anything from *umeboshi* (pickled Japanese apricots) to tuna salad to *karashimentaiko* (spicy salted cod roe) or wrapped in anything from nori to *shiso* to marinated *konbu*. Or, as Hitomi likes to do, the stuffing is mixed directly into the rice for a more interesting texture and presentation. Sometimes the "balls" are shaped into triangles, as shown in the photograph.

Yet another variation is to crisp the rice balls (or triangles), top with a miso glaze and wrap with a shiso leaf, as is shown in the photograph to the right. If making this crispy, miso-coated version, the rice balls can be made ahead, and then baked in the oven just before serving.

MAKES 4 RICE BALLS/TRIANGLES

⅓ **cup (45 g) blanched, slivered almonds**
¼ **cup (15 g) small dried sardines (chirimen) (optional)**
½ **recipe White Rice (page 28)**
Salt

1. Toast the slivered almonds and dried sardines together in a small skillet over medium-high heat until the almonds turn golden brown and the fish become dry and crispy, 3 to 5 minutes. Let cool slightly.

2. In a large bowl, stir to combine the toasted almonds, sardines and just-cooked rice.

3. With damp, lightly salted hands, use ½ cup (85 g) of the hot rice mixture to form a ball or triangle. Repeat with remaining rice. If the rice begins to stick to your palms, re-moisten and salt your palms as necessary.

4. The Onigiri can be served now while still warm, or at room temperature. Or, use to make the Miso-Glazed Onigiri (recipe on opposite page).

5. To store leftover unglazed Onigiri, wrap tightly in plastic and continue manipulating the wrapped rice to emphasize the shape of the rice ball or triangle. Refrigerate or freeze.

Cooking Tips *Onigiri is a perfect way to use up leftover rice—wrapped tightly in plastic wrap, the rice ball will keep well in either the refrigerator or freezer.*

Shaped into a smaller size, the rice balls also make a nice bite-size hors d'oeuvre. (When shaping the rice balls into whatever size desired, be sure to use hot rice, as it helps the rice stick together better.)

If the dried miniature sardines (chirimen) seem too off-putting, simply omit them. The recipe will still be delicious.

Miso-Glazed Onigiri

Variation: Miso-Glazed Onigiri

4 Almond Rice Onigiri (page 72)
4 shiso leaves (optional)

MISO GLAZE
4 tablespoons miso
3 tablespoons saké
1 teaspoon sugar

1. Preheat the oven to 400°F (200°C).
2. To make the Miso Glaze, whisk together the ingredients in a small bowl until combined. Set aside.
3. Place the Onigiri on a lightly oiled baking sheet and bake for 10 minutes, or until crisp and lightly browned. (If using pre-made Onigiri that were previously refrigerated or frozen, bring to room temperature before baking.)
4. Remove the baking sheet and set the oven to broil. Brush the top side of each Onigiri with the Miso Glaze to coat evenly, and then broil for 3 to 5 minutes, watching closely since the glaze burns easily.
5. For the best flavor, let cool briefly, then wrap each Onigiri in a *shiso* leaf, if using, before serving.

Chicken and Vegetable Rice Medley
Takikomi Gohan

This is a very homestyle dish—meaning the "medley" of ingredients used to flavor the rice vary greatly from one household to the next. This is the version Hitomi made for me on my first night back in Japan.

SERVES 6 AS A SIDE DISH

1½ cups (90 g) sliced assorted fresh mushrooms (such as shimeji, eringi or shiitake)

2 tablespoons soy sauce, divided

2 tablespoons saké, divided

1 boneless, skinless chicken thigh, cubed

One 3 x 5-in (7.5 x 12.75-cm) sheet fried tofu (abura-age), rolled in paper towel to remove excess oil, thinly sliced

2 regular cups (440 g) (if using stovetop method) or 2 "rice" cups (300 g) (if using rice cooker) uncooked short-grain white "sushi" rice, washed and drained (see "Rice Making 101," page 28)

2 cups (500 ml) Fish Stock (page 26) for stovetop method or, if using rice cooker, about 1½ cups (360 ml) (enough to reach 1.5-cup line)

¼ cup (65 g) canned soybeans, drained and rinsed

⅓ cup (50 g) diced carrot

Cooking Tips *For a vegetarian option, simply omit the chicken and use Vegetarian Stock (page 27). You'll still have a hearty meal as the mushrooms give this dish a very rich, earthy flavor.*

If she has it on hand, Hitomi will add cubed satoimo (taro root) to the rice. If using taro root, let it marinate in the same bag as the chicken and fried tofu.

Wash and drain the rice and then let rest while preparing the remaining ingredients.

Special Equipment *Rice cooker or 4-quart (3.75-liter) pot with tight-fitting lid*

1. Put the sliced mushrooms in a small resealable plastic bag with 1½ teaspoons of the soy sauce and 1½ teaspoons of the saké. Set aside. In a separate bag, add the chicken and fried tofu with 1½ teaspoons each of the soy sauce and saké. Let both bags marinate 10 minutes, tossing occasionally.

2. You can make this dish either on the stovetop or in a rice cooker, as shown in the photographs at right. To cook on the stovetop, combine the rice, Fish Stock and remaining 1 tablespoon each of the soy sauce and saké in a 4-quart (3.75-liter) pot. Bring to a boil over high heat. Proceed to Step 4.

3. To make this dish in a rice cooker, place the rice in the cooker and pour the Fish Stock to the "1.5-cup" line. Add remaining 1 tablespoon each of the soy sauce and saké (the liquid level should now be at the "1.8-cup" line.) Do not add liquid to reach the "2-cup" line as the ingredients will release moisture while cooking.

4. Layer the following on top of the rice in this order: 1) the marinated chicken mixture, 2) the soybeans, 3) the marinated mushrooms and 4) the carrots.

5. If cooking on the stovetop, cover, reduce the heat to the lowest setting and cook 35 minutes, or until the rice is tender and all the liquid has been absorbed. Remove from the heat and let rest 10 minutes before taking off the cover. Fluff before serving.

6. If cooking with a rice cooker, cook according to the manufacturer's directions. Fluff before serving.

Chicken and Vegetable Rice Medley

Black and White Rice
Kuromai

Kuromai, or black rice (also sometimes called "forbidden rice"), is an heirloom variety of rice known for its health properties. Most commonly mixed with white rice, it is usually used only in small amounts because, on its own, it's considered by many to be too *katai* (hard) to comfortably digest. When cooked together with white rice, the dish will have an overall purple-ish hue.

SERVES 6 AS A SIDE DISH

1¾ cups (385 g) uncooked short-grain white "sushi" rice, washed and drained (see "Rice Making 101," page 28)
¼ cup (50 g) black rice
½ teaspoon salt
2¼ cups (565 ml) water

1. Combine the short-grain and black rice, salt, and water in a 4-quart (3.75-liter) pot over medium-high heat. Bring to a boil, cover, reduce the heat to the lowest setting and cook 15 minutes, or until the rice is tender and all the liquid has been absorbed.

2. Remove from the heat and let rest 10 minutes before taking off the cover. Fluff before serving.

Cooking Tip *For a dramatic color presentation, I like to serve a fried egg, sunny-side up, on top of the purple-ish rice, garnished with thinly sliced chives.*

Rice with Green Peas
Mame Gohan

Upon returning from an early-morning run through the streets of Iwaki, I found Hiromi surprisingly awake (late hours at the restaurant and night-owl tendencies have made mornings rather unfamiliar territory for her). She was already busy at work in the kitchen, putting even more than her usual effort into the delicious late-afternoon lunches she'd been spoiling me with. As I soon found out, the reason for this extravagance was that Ms. Sato, her friend and travel agent, was invited over to discuss plans for their upcoming trip to Scandinavia. In addition to the many dishes on the menu, Hiromi took the time to enhance the traditional plain white rice with beautiful green peas at the peak of their season. Despite its simplicity, this recipe is surprisingly flavorful.

SERVES 6 AS A SIDE DISH

2 cups (440 g) uncooked short-grain white "sushi" rice, washed and drained (see "Rice Making 101," page 28)

1 tablespoon mirin

½ teaspoon salt

2¼ cups (565 ml) water

1 cup (142 g) fresh or frozen green peas

Cooking Tips *Some cooks blanch the peas before steaming, but I like to add them raw, preferring the "pop" of slightly underdone peas. If freshly shucked spring peas are unavailable, an equal amount of frozen peas may be substituted.*

When in season, try using fresh fava beans—blanched to remove their outer skins (see instructions, page 59)—in place of the peas.

1. Combine the rice, mirin, salt and water in a 4-quart (3.75-liter) pot over high heat. Stir in the peas. Bring to a boil, cover, reduce the heat to the lowest setting and cook 15 minutes, or until the rice is tender and all the liquid has been absorbed.

2. Remove from the heat and let rest 10 minutes before taking off the cover. Fluff before serving.

Miso-Filled Rice Patties
Café Mikunia Konetsuke

I discovered this recipe when I stumbled upon Café Mikunia, a minimalist café on the outskirts of Obuse (just outside of Nagano, Obuse is one of my favorite towns in Japan). I mentioned to the owner that I was doing research for a cookbook, and she seemed more than eager to help. Racking her brain for what she considered *kyodo-ryori* (local cuisine), she soon brought out these delicious rice patties, prepared within minutes, for me to try. Not only was I taken aback by her hospitality, I was thoroughly impressed with what she had prepared.

This version of Konetsuke reminds me of a peppermint patty: Two layers of rice surrounding a thin layer of miso. Packaged miso works well, but this tastes even better if made with Hitomi's Peanut Miso (page 33).

You might have noticed that there is another *konetsuke* recipe in this book (see page 89). A regional term, it simply refers to any dish that combines rice and flour.

MAKES 8 PATTIES (SERVES 4 AS A LIGHT LUNCH WITH A SALAD OR VEGETABLE)

1 recipe White Rice (page 28)
¼ cup (36 g) all-purpose flour
½ cup (128 g) miso or Peanut Miso (page 33), divided
½ cup (125 ml) oil, divided

Cooking Tip *I recommend cooking two patties at time. Though four patties will easily fit in most skillets, they soak up too much oil so that when you flip them there isn't enough oil remaining, causing the patties to burn.*

1. Combine the hot, cooked rice and flour in a large bowl.

2. Have a small bowl of water and a small bowl of salt on hand for dipping your hands into before forming each patty. To form the rice patties, follow the illustrated steps on the opposite page.

3. Heat 2 tablespoons of the oil in a 10-inch (25-cm) skillet over medium-high heat. Fry 2 patties until crisp and starting to brown, 2 to 3 minutes per side. Transfer to a paper towel–lined baking sheet and repeat with the remaining oil and patties. Serve warm.

Forming the Rice Patties

1. With damp, lightly salted hands, gently press ¼ cup (40 g) of the rice-mixture to form a circle about 3 inches (7.5 cm) across and between ¼ and ½ inch (6 mm and 1.25 cm) thick.

2. Place the patty on a wax paper–lined cookie sheet and repeat with remaining rice to form 16 patties.

3. Spread 1 tablespoon of miso over eight of the patties.

4. Top each of the 8 miso-covered patties with the remaining 8 plain patties. With damp hands, form a rice patty "sandwich" by gently yet firmly cupping the rice and pressing to seal the edges. Repeat with the remaining patties until all are sealed. (You may need to dampen your hands again to prevent the rice from sticking to you.)

A Cook's Journey to Japan

Sushi Rice with Toppings
Barazushi

*B*arazushi is a very homestyle, casual type of sushi noted for its informal presentation and preparation. Although found all over Japan, it's often under different aliases, such as *chirashizushi* and *gomokuzushi*.

Chirashizushi is probably heard most commonly, named after the word *chirasu*, meaning "to scatter." In Osaka, they call it *barazushi* (which is where I was taught to make it), named after *barasu*, meaning "to break something into many pieces." And finally, gomokuzushi. While *go* literally means "five," the dish itself is not limited to five toppings. Instead, it simply means not only two or three, but many.

Be creative with the combinations. Cucumber, shiitake and crab are nice together, as well as shrimp and avocado. If unable to find lotus root, try substituting water chestnuts.

Barazushi makes a great side dish, as well as a welcome addition to any potluck or event where a family-style dish is needed.

SERVES 4

5 dried shiitake mushrooms (about ½ oz/15g)

½ cup (125 ml) boiling water

¼ cup (36 g) peeled and diced lotus root or water chestnuts

¼ cup (40 g) trimmed and sliced green beans

2 tablespoons water

2 tablespoons soy sauce

1 tablespoon sugar

2 tablespoons peeled and diced carrot

2 tablespoons diced burdock (optional)

1 recipe Sushi Rice (page 29)

½ cup (55 g) Golden Thread Eggs (page 32)

2 tablespoons slivered nori

PICKLING MIXTURE

¼ cup (65 ml) rice wine vinegar

2 tablespoons sugar

1 teaspoon soy sauce

1. Place the dried shiitake in a small bowl and pour in the ½ cup of boiling water. Cover with plastic wrap and let stand until tender, about 30 minutes.

2. To make the Pickling Mixture, combine the ingredients in a small bowl. Set aside.

3. Bring a small saucepan of water to a boil. Add the lotus root and cook for 2 minutes. Using a slotted spoon, immediately transfer the lotus root to the Pickling Mixture. (Do not discard the cooking water.) Let the lotus root pickle while preparing the remaining ingredients.

4. Return the same small saucepan of water to a boil. Add the green beans and blanch for 1 minute. Drain, and immediately plunge into ice water until cool. (This stops the delicate beans from continuing to cook.) Drain, and set aside.

5. When tender, drain the mushrooms, reserving the soaking liquid. Trim off and discard the stems and slice the mushrooms thinly (you should have about ¼ cup/40 g). Set aside.

6. Bring the 2 tablespoons water, soy sauce, sugar and 4 tablespoons of the reserved mushroom water just to a boil in the same small saucepan. Add the diced carrots and burdock and sliced shiitake mushrooms and simmer on low until tender and most of the liquid has been absorbed, about 10 minutes. Drain.

7. To assemble, drain the lotus root from the Pickling Mixture it was marinating in. In a large serving bowl, gently stir together the Sushi Rice, lotus root, green beans and carrot-burdock-shiitake-mixture. Top with the Golden Thread Eggs and slivered nori. Serve warm or at room temperature.

Cooking Tip *Both the lotus root and burdock will quickly discolor after being cut. To prevent this from happening, place in a small bowl of water with a tablespoon or two of lemon juice or white vinegar until ready to use.*

Chicken 'n Rice Stew Keihan

This is a traditional recipe from Atsuko's childhood home, the island of Amami Oshima, situated just off the southernmost tip of Kyushu and just north of the famed island of Okinawa. It's also the island's signature dish. When the emperor visited Amami Oshima, this is the meal he was served. Even after years of living away from home, Atsuko's native hospitality is intact—anytime a guest is invited into her home for dinner, she prepares this dish (talk about treating your guests like royalty!). Atsuko must have been entertaining a lot by the time I visited her because as soon as Raito, the eldest of Atsuko's three boys, found out Keihan was on the menu for dinner that night, he immediately groaned, "Not again!" Yet most of his dissatisfaction must have come from typical teenage angst because as soon as the chicken was done stewing, the three boys huddled over the leftover carcass, chopsticks in hand, voraciously devouring every last bit of flesh left clinging to the bird.

Keihan is simply clear chicken broth poured over stewed chicken meat and white rice that is then "dressed up" with an assortment of colorful garnishes: yellow zest, red ginger, green onions . . . this is a gorgeous dish! Most of the preparation can be completed a day ahead—only the slivered egg pancakes (called *kinshitamago* after *kinshi*, meaning "golden thread") and rice are best made the day served. If you're in a hurry, go ahead and use purchased chicken broth and pre-cooked chicken. Whole, rotisserie chickens that are common in larger grocery stores provide a convenient alternative that drastically cuts down on the cooking time.

SERVES 6

1 whole chicken, about 5 lbs (2.25 kg)
4 quarts (3.75 liters) water
2 tablespoons salt, divided
5 tablespoons soy sauce, preferably light, divided
1 chicken bouillon cube (optional)
1 tablespoon sugar
1 recipe White Rice (page 28)
Toasted sesame seeds, for garnish (see "Toasting Sesame Seeds," page 16)

CONDIMENTS

1 recipe Marinated Mushrooms, thinly sliced (page 31) (reserve mushroom soaking liquid)
Nori, slivered
Green onions (scallions), finely chopped, green part only
1 recipe Golden Thread Eggs (page 32)
¼ to ½ cup (34 to 68 g) yellow pickled daikon (takuan), minced
Citrus zest, thinly sliced (e.g., lemon, orange, lime, yuzu, sudachi—whatever is in season and you have on hand)
Red pickled ginger slivers (beni shoga)

MAKE AHEAD:

1. Place the chicken in a large stockpot. Pour in the water, or enough to just cover the chicken. Bring to a boil. Reduce the heat to medium-low and simmer, uncovered, for 1 hour. While the chicken cooks, skim off the *aku* (foam) as it appears on the surface of the water. This ensures the broth will be clear.

2. Reduce the heat to low, add 1 tablespoon of the salt, cover, and simmer 1 hour more.

3. Transfer the chicken from the stockpot to a work surface, reserving the broth. Remove the skin and meat from the bones—the chicken will be quite tender and easily break apart. Shred the meat—be careful, it's hot! Set the shredded chicken aside. Discard the bones.

4. You should have about 3 quarts (3 liters) of chicken broth left in the pot (use water or canned chicken broth to make up any difference). Add the remaining 1 tablespoon of salt and 3 tablespoons of soy sauce. Stir to combine and taste. If you feel the broth is too watery, add the optional chicken bouillon cube and stir until dissolved. Set aside.

5. Place the shredded chicken in the same saucepan used for making the Marinated Mushrooms. Add the remaining mushroom soaking liquid and, if necessary, fill with water until the level of the liquid is just below the chicken. Stir in the sugar and the remaining 2 tablespoons of soy sauce. Simmer over medium-low heat until most of the liquid has been absorbed, 10 to 15 minutes. Pour into a small bowl and set the marinated chicken meat aside.

6. The broth and marinated chicken can be used now or refrigerated for up to 2 days.

DAY OF:

7. If the broth and marinated chicken have been refrigerated, reheat on the stovetop over low heat, in separate containers, until heated through. Bring the Marinated Mushrooms to room temperature.

8. Prepare the Golden Thread Eggs and White Rice.

SERVING:

9. On six individual plates, arrange the chicken, sliced Marinated Mushrooms, nori, green onions and Golden Thread Eggs in small piles along the outer edge of the plate, and the *takuan*, citrus zest and *beni shoga* in the middle.

10. Divide the rice among six soup bowls, top with broth, and serve with the plated chicken and condiments, inviting each guest to top his or her bowl with the ingredients of his or her choice. Provide toasted sesame seeds for garnish.

FRied Soba NoodLes and Rice
Soba Meshi

Although Hiromi was the first person to introduce me to it, *Soba Meshi* actually comes from Kobe, a modern port city south of Kyoto, famous for the devastating earthquake of 1995 and the expensive beef that is raised there. Like most great inventions, this dish came about by accident: There was a small noodle shop on the outskirts of Kobe that wasn't getting much business. Playing around one day, the owners ended up frying rice and soba noodles together. Customers liked it, so it was put on the menu. Word got out about the new dish, more and more people visited the shop, and the rest, as they say, is history.

Of course, I had to visit, too. When I walked into the small, dinerlike restaurant, there was a row of four women crowded around the counter—which served double-duty as both the cooking grill as well as their plates! The cook stands on one side of the counter preparing orders and then simply slides the finished dish over to the customers' side of the long, flat grill. Traditionally, the meal is served with small metal spatulas to be used as forks, but the size doesn't seem quite right—too small to function as a real spatula, and too big to fit in your mouth. Plus, the spatula leaves an unpleasant metallic aftertaste. I much preferred the *gaijin* (foreigner) alternative: a spoon.

The original Soba Meshi recipe, from which the restaurant has yet to stray during the last fifty years, adds only ground beef, onions and cabbage as "fillers." Not limited by the financial constraints from which this dish was born, Hiromi's version—with the addition of pork, green peppers and mushrooms—is a bit more sophisticated. I've provided her version here.

SERVES 4

1 teaspoon oil

½ lb (250 g) ground pork

2 cups (122 g) shredded cabbage

1 cup (70 g) diced fresh eringi mushrooms (from about 1 whole), or other favorite mushrooms

½ cup (60 g) diced green bell pepper

½ cup (75 g) diced onion

1 tablespoon saké

½ recipe White Rice (page 28)

Two 5½-oz (156-g) packages fresh or defrosted frozen yaki soba noodles, room temperature

Sliced green onion (scallion), for garnish

Leftover tempura bits (tenkasu) (see page 24) (optional), for garnish

SAUCE

¾ cup (185 ml) store-bought yaki soba sauce

¼ cup (65 ml) ketchup

1 teaspoon fresh ground pepper

1. To make the Sauce, combine the ingredients in a small bowl. Set aside.

2. Add the oil to a large skillet over medium-high heat. When hot, add the ground pork and cook through, 3 to 5 minutes. Using a slotted spoon, transfer the meat to a bowl. Drain the excess fat from the skillet.

3. In the same skillet, over medium-high heat, add the cabbage, mushrooms, green pepper, onion and saké. Sauté until tender, but not browned, 3 to 5 minutes. Transfer the veggies to the bowl holding the meat.

4. Add a bit more oil to the skillet, if necessary. Sauté the rice and noodles over medium-high heat. As you cook and stir the noodles, break them into bite-size pieces with the edge of a spoon. When warmed through and starting to crisp, about 5 minutes, add the cooked meat and veggies and stir to combine. Pour in the Sauce and stir until everything is evenly coated—you may not choose to use all the Sauce, depending on how "saucy" you want the dish to be. Heat through and garnish with the green onion and tempura bits, if using. Serve warm.

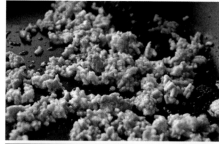

Cooking Tips *This recipe is great for using up leftover cooked rice. When it comes to the noodles, be sure to use* yaki soba *(thin, yellow Chinese noodles made from flour and egg), and not Japanese* soba *noodles made from buckwheat flour. Yaki soba can be found in the refrigerated section of large Asian markets. For this recipe, you'll need plain, unseasoned yaki soba. Discard the flavor packets that frequently come packaged with the noodles or save for another use.*

Be careful not to overcook the green pepper as it adds a desired crunch. The black pepper is meant to add a little bit of heat. Hiromi likes to use Otafuku-brand yaki soba sauce.

Soba Meshi *gets its dark color from the sauce it is tossed with, not the degree to which the vegetables, rice and noodles are cooked. When preparing this dish, there is no need to "brown" each of its components.*

If eringi mushrooms are unavailable, use whatever variety of mushroom you prefer.

Ginger Rice *Shoga Gohan*

Both Hiromi and I love ginger, so we enjoyed this dish often during the time I was staying with her. This is probably why the smell of *Shoga Gohan* cooking is, for me, incredibly reminiscent of Japan.

With the ginger flavor far from overwhelming, this recipe offers a great way to spruce up plain white rice, especially when the ginger's flavor is meant to complement the main dish. Try serving with the Sesame Fried Chicken (page 95), Seasoned Fish Hamburgers (page 111) or Squid with Edamame (page 122).

Hiromi prefers to use the delicate *shin shoga*, or young ginger, when making this dish, but I still prefer the bite of the more common, mature ginger. Whichever variety of ginger is used, it is first washed in salt water to remove the *aku* (harsh taste) before using.

SERVES 6 AS A SIDE DISH

One 3-in (7.5-cm) piece fresh ginger root, peeled and slivered
1 teaspoon salt
2 cups (440 g) uncooked short-grain white "sushi" rice, washed and drained (see "Rice Making 101," page 28)
2 cups (500 ml) plus 2 tablespoons Fish Stock (page 26)
1½ tablespoons saké
1½ teaspoons mirin
1½ teaspoons soy sauce
½ teaspoon salt

1. Combine the ginger and salt in a small bowl and let rest 10 minutes.
2. Rinse off the ginger and drain well. Do not squeeze dry.
3. Combine the rice, Fish Stock, saké, mirin, soy sauce and salt in a 4-quart (3.75-liter) pot over high heat. Top with the ginger slices. Bring to a boil, cover, reduce the heat to the lowest setting and cook 15 minutes, or until the rice is tender and all the liquid has been absorbed. Remove from the heat and let rest 10 minutes before taking off the cover. Fluff before serving.

Cooking Tip *If desired, add thinly sliced fried tofu sheets (abura-age) to the rice pot before cooking.*

Brown Rice with Red Beans Azuki Gohan

In rural areas of Japan, it's not uncommon to find stalls on the side of the road where do-it-yourself hulling machines will quickly turn brown rice white.

While visiting a friend's home one evening, I happened to notice her mom programming the rice cooker for breakfast the next morning. Seeing that I was taking an interest in her kitchen habits, she took great pride in showing me the stash of fresh brown rice she uses, personally harvested from her father's rice paddy. I soon realized that what she was even more excited to show me was her personal, miniature home-hulling machine which effortlessly turned the beautiful brown rice white in under a minute!

A few days later, I was fortunate to find myself staying at a youth hostel near the famous Dogo Onsen in Shikoku where they offered three(!) varieties of rice with your meal: plain White Rice (page 28), Barley Rice (recipe on this page) and this protein-rich Brown Rice with Red Beans. What follows is a simple variation of the youth hostel's offering.

SERVES 4 TO 6 AS A SIDE DISH

2 cups (440 g) uncooked short-grain brown rice, washed and drained (see "Rice Making 101," page 28)
3 cups (750 ml) water
½ teaspoon salt
¼ cup (54 g) dried adzuki beans, soaked for 24 hours

1. Bring the rice, water, salt and beans to a boil in a 4-quart (3.75-liter) pot over medium-high heat. Cover, reduce the heat to the lowest setting, and simmer for 40 minutes, or until the rice is tender and all the liquid has been absorbed.

2. Remove from the heat and let rest 10 minutes before taking off the cover. Fluff before serving.

Cooking Tips *If you're short on time, you can use ¾ cup (195 g) canned adzuki beans in place of the dried. But the beans will be a bit mushier, have a darker color, and won't infuse their slight red hue into the rice.*

It's best not to prepare this recipe in a rice cooker unless it is equipped with a brown rice setting.

While not typical to add salt when making white rice, it is sometimes included when making brown rice as this recipe reflects.

Barley Rice Mugi Gohan

This rice-barley combo is typically served with cold soups, like *Hiyajiru*, a specialty of the southern town of Miyazaki. While none of the cold soups I tried are on my "must-eat-again" list, this rice dish, on the other hand, is. The barley adds an extra element of texture and nuttiness that provides a welcome change of pace from the everyday plain white version.

Try serving alongside Burdock Soup (page 60), Braised Spare Ribs (page 102) or Spicy Carrot and Burdock Root (page 127).

Whenever I talk to people about *mugi* (barley), their first reaction is to make a funny face and comment on its "unpleasant" smell (although I've never been bothered by it). To offset barley's strong aroma, barley rice is commonly prepared with a larger ratio of plain white rice to the amount of barley used.

SERVES 6 AS A SIDE DISH

1¾ cups (385 g) uncooked short-grain white "sushi" rice, washed and drained (see "Rice Making 101," page 28)
3 cups (750 ml) water
½ teaspoon salt
¾ cup (114 g) quick pearled barley

1. Bring the rice, water and salt to a boil in a 4-quart (3.75-liter) pot over medium-high heat. Stir in the barley, cover, reduce the heat to the lowest setting and cook 15 minutes, or until the rice is tender and all the liquid has been absorbed.

2. Remove from the heat and let rest 10 minutes before taking off the cover. Fluff before serving.

Cooking Tip *When making this rice, do not use a saucepan smaller than 4 quarts (3.75 liters) as the barley has a tendency to boil over during cooking.*

Soy Sauce Udon Noodles

K otohira is a quaint town in the Kagawa prefecture of Shikoku known for Kompira-san, a shrine housed on top of a mini-mountain made famous by the over 1,300 steep steps leading up to it. Although that's a lot of steps, and many *are* quite steep, it's still rather endearing to observe how the Japanese exaggerate this effort. Each climber is outfitted as for a summit attempt of Mt. Everest, geared up with a walking stick, fan, shade umbrella, camera and towel wrapped around the neck—or in hand—for dabbing away the very first drop of sweat.

The town is also known for its *udon*, perfect for re-fueling after a day's climb. A bowl of hot noodles comes complete with fried tempura bits, sliced chives and dried bonito fish flakes dancing on top. This simple combination is especially good when you have great-tasting udon noodles that you want to savor, not mask.

SERVES 4

One 8-oz (250-g) package dried udon noodles

½ cup (42 g) green onions (scallions), thinly sliced (from about 2 whole)

½ cup (25 g) tempura bits (tenkasu) (see page 24)

½ cup (5 g) dried bonito fish flakes (katsuobushi)

¼ cup (65 ml) soy sauce, preferably light

1. Bring a pot of water to a boil. Cook the *udon* according to package instructions (generally about 8 to 10 minutes). Drain, rinse, and drain again. Set aside.

2. Divide the hot noodles among four bowls. Decorate with the green onions, tempura bits and bonito flakes. Drizzle 1 tablespoon of the soy sauce over the top of each bowl, or to taste.

Cooking Tip *To serve the noodles as authentically as the noodle shops in Shikoku, warm the bowls before serving, following the tip on page 52.*

Sanuki Udon

Sanuki Udon *is famous throughout Japan. Anytime I mentioned I was headed to Takamatsu, without fail, the first suggestion anyone would offer was to eat these famous noodles. (Sanuki is the old name for this area of Shikoku.)*

The people of Sanuki (referred to as Sanuki-ko) are said to eat udon no less than once a day. As the Sanuki-saying goes: Udon wa betsu bara. Betsu bara *translates to "separate stomach," and is usually used as the excuse for eating dessert after an already filling meal. But in Sanuki, it's udon they always have more room for! The flavorful noodles are most often eaten plain, save for a few colorful choices of garnishes: wakame, mentaiko, curry, egg, mayonnaise, tempura bits, sesame seeds, or ground ginger (see Soy Sauce Udon Noodles, recipe on this page).*

Tachigui udon (train station food stalls where you eat while standing) are especially common, since udon is truly FAST food—a real connoisseur can proudly slurp down an entire bowl of noodles in less than three minutes!

Pan-Fried Noodles
Yaki Udon

These pan-fried noodles are a quick, cheap, easy dish that is eaten all over Japan. For many Japanese, it is comfort food. It was for me, too, while living there. In Japan, the refrigerator section of my local grocery store boasted a wide selection of fresh *udon* noodles: different brands, different flavorings. You'd be hard-pressed to find a grocery cart without a pack or two on its way home to be turned into a quick dinner.

Similar to Fried Soba Noodles and Rice (page 84), fresh noodles—opposed to dried— are used for making Pan-Fried Noodles. The noodles often come packaged with their own seasoning packet (I said this dish was easy), but with a few simple seasonings of your own (garlic, pepper, onions), the dish is effortlessly made that much more flavorful. The great thing about Yaki Udon is that it benefits from your personal touch. Play around with the add-ins, adjusting to your taste preference and for what ingredients you have on hand. This peppery version is how my friend, Atusko, likes to make it.

Pan-Fried Noodles

SERVES 2 TO 4

Four 6²/₃-oz (188-g) packages fresh or defrosted frozen udon noodles, room temperature

2 tablespoons oil

1 onion, thinly sliced

2 carrots, peeled and chopped

2 cloves garlic, thinly sliced

4 green onions (scallions), sliced on the bias

SAUCE

4 tablespoons soy sauce

4 teaspoons sugar

1½ teaspoons salt

1½ teaspoons pepper

1. To make the Sauce, whisk together the ingredients in a small bowl. Set aside.

2. Loosen the clump of noodles, pulling apart each individual strand. (If the noodles came packaged with a seasoning packet, discard or save for another use.)

3. Add the oil to a large skillet over medium-high heat. When hot, add the onion and sauté until soft and transparent, about 3 minutes. Add the carrots and continue to cook until they start to soften, 3 to 5 minutes. Add the garlic and sauté until fragrant, about 30 seconds. Add the noodles and, stirring constantly, cook until heated through, about 2 minutes. Pour in the Sauce and stir until fully combined, about 1 minute. Off heat, toss in the sliced green onions and serve.

Fried Rice Logs
Konetsuke Reiko-Style

When I asked Reiko about *Konetsuke*, she was of course already familiar with this local specialty. A quick trip to the kitchen yielded a dish with a few personal touches of her own.

As Reiko soon convinced me, this is a great way to use up leftover rice. Since the rice logs need to be frozen before cooking, keep a stockpile in the freezer until ready to use.

For another take on Konetsuke, check out the recipe for Miso-Filled Rice Patties (page 78).

SERVES 6 AS AN APPETIZER

1 recipe White Rice (page 28)
¼ cup (36 g) all-purpose flour
½ cup (64 g) toasted sesame seeds (see "Toasting Sesame Seeds," page 16)
½ cup (125 ml) soy sauce
¼ cup (50 g) sugar

1. Let the rice cool down just enough so that's easy to handle. (It's helpful to form the logs while the rice is still warm as the steam from the just-cooked rice helps the logs stick together.)

2. Mix together the rice, flour and sesame seeds in a large bowl. Divide the mixture into three sections and with lightly floured hands, shape into three logs, each about 7½ x 1½ inches (19 x 3.75 cm). Wrap tightly in plastic wrap and freeze until set, about 4 hours.

3. When ready to cook, let the frozen logs stand at room temperature for 30 minutes, or until able to easily slice with a sharp knife. The logs should still be partially frozen and firm enough to hold their shape.

4. While the logs are defrosting, whisk the soy sauce and sugar in a small bowl. (The longer the sauce sits, the better the sugar will dissolve.) Set aside.

5. Slice the frozen rice logs into ½-inch (1.25-cm)-thick pieces.

6. Add 2 tablespoons of the soy mixture to a 10-inch (25-cm) skillet over low heat and bring just to a simmer. Add enough of the rice pieces to comfortably fill the pan and cook until warmed through, about 2 minutes per side. Use a spatula to gently flip. Repeat with the remaining sauce and pieces. Serve warm.

Cooking Tips *The trick to perfectly cooking the sliced rice logs lies in the soy sauce mixture. If you add the rice pieces to the sauce too early, they will soak up too much of the liquid and taste overly salty. Instead, as the mixture cooks, the sauce reduces and turns syrupy, which is the consistency and flavor you are going for!*

If you have any unused sauce left over, reduce until thick and syrupy and drizzle over the konetsuke *just before serving.*

Cold Sesame Noodle Salad
Hiyashi Chuka

The first time I ate this dish was as an *ekiben* (station meal) I bought before boarding the old-fashioned, one-car train traveling through the countryside along the Shimanto Gawa (erroneously considered the last free flowing river in Japan), headed towards the town of Uwajima on the southern island of Shikoku. The train "stations" we stopped at were nothing more than makeshift wind shields—no buildings, no employees—and no more than a small platform where waiting passengers could board. Just like a bus, you took a ticket when you boarded and paid the conductor as you got off.

I was almost too distracted by the beautiful scenery to taste the incredibly simple homemade meal that I bought for its familiarity—cold spaghetti-like noodles topped with sliced ham, cucumber and egg, then dressed with spicy yellow mustard and a sesame-sweetened soy sauce. Surprised by how much flavor came from such an everyday combination, I thought I had stumbled upon something truly unique. It was only later, as I walked through the streets of various towns, that I saw plastic replicas of the garnished noodles advertised in every restaurant window. While it may not be obscure, it is definitely delicious.

Hiyashi Chuka is a Chinese-influenced cold noodle dish (*chuka* means "Chinese") commonly eaten throughout Japan during the hot summer months. As with most dishes in Japan, the actual ingredients vary depending on the area in which the meal is served. When my friend moved from a city just outside of Tokyo to the northern city of Iwaki, she was served Hiyashi Chuka as part of her school lunch, but garnished with a large dollop of mayonnaise—a first for her to see!

SERVES 4 FOR LUNCH OR AS A LIGHT SUPPER

One 8-oz (250-g) package dried chuka soba or spaghetti noodles

4 teaspoons red pickled ginger slivers (beni shoga), divided

4 teaspoons mayonnaise, divided

2 teaspoons prepared hot mustard (Japanese, Chinese or Colman's) (optional)

TOPPINGS

1 cup (130 g) sugar snap peas, blanched, plunged into ice water and drained

½ cup (70 g) thinly sliced Marinated Mushrooms (page 31)

½ cup (55 g) Golden Thread Eggs (page 32)

1 tomato, sliced into 12 thin wedges

One 1¼-in (3-cm)-thick slice deli ham, thinly sliced

DRESSING

½ cup (125 ml) rice wine vinegar

¼ cup (65 ml) soy sauce

1 tablespoon sugar

1 teaspoon sesame oil

2 tablespoons ground toasted sesame seeds (see "Toasting Sesame Seeds," page 16)

1. To make the Dressing, in a small bowl stir together the rice wine vinegar, soy sauce, sugar and sesame oil until the sugar is dissolved. Stir in the ground sesame seeds and set aside.

2. Bring a large pot of water to a boil. Add the chuka soba, return the water to a boil, and cook according to package instructions, about 2 minutes. Drain. Rinse under cold water. Drain again.

3. To assemble, divide the noodles among four shallow bowls. Arrange each of the prepared toppings in five colorful strips, from the center to the edge of the bowl. Place a small mound of the pickled ginger and a small dollop of the mayonnaise in the center where the toppings meet. For added heat, place a small dollop of the mustard on the rim of the serving dish, if using.

4. Serve with the Dressing on the side, allowing each diner to dress the noodles to taste.

Cooking Tip *The great thing about this dish is that most of the ingredients can be prepared ahead of time so that all you have to do is boil the noodles and then assemble the dish just before serving. Though the station meal version I enjoyed in Uwajima had the spicy mustard mixed into the dressing, I like to place the hot mustard (karashi) on the rim of the serving dish to allow diners to better control the level of heat in each bite.*

CHAPTER 4

PouLtry and Meat

During one of my very first weeks in Japan—brand new to the language and culture—my boss and her husband graciously took me out to dinner to a *yakiniku* (grilled meat) restaurant. As I was just biting into a hot-off-the-grill cut of meat, I noticed the two of them staring at me, eagerly anticipating my reaction. Confused by their stares, I was soon informed that I was eating *cow's tongue*, and they wanted to know how I liked it.

That is how I learned that Japanese cuisine is not all about sushi.

As the home of Kobe beef, it should come as no surprise that there are some delicious meat and poultry recipes in Japan. *Shabu-shabu, sukiyaki* . . . these are the dishes Japan is famous for. But beyond these respectable tourist favorites, there are a number of simple, homestyle dishes that are feeding families on any given weeknight. Included in this chapter are some of my favorites.

Sesame Fried Chicken
Tori Kara-age

Kara-age, Japanese fried chicken, is one of the most popular "snack" foods in Japan. You are guaranteed to find it at any street festival, as an addition to most *o-bento* (lunch boxes), and in the "grab 'n go" prepared foods section of larger grocery stores. But it is Atusko's masterful version—perfectly tender chicken on the inside and a crispy, not-too-oily exterior with just the right amount of sesame flavor—that I look forward to on each visit.

The chicken is best if left to marinate two hours to overnight, so plan accordingly. Atsuko's recipe doesn't call for ginger juice in the marinade, although many Kara-age recipes do. I've included it as an optional ingredient. (I love all things ginger, but Atsuko's recipe is plenty flavorful without.) If you're especially fond of ginger, though, you might want to give it a try.

SERVES 4 AS A MAIN MEAL; 6 AS A SIDE DISH

1 lb (500 g) boneless, skin-on chicken thighs, cut into 1-in (2.5-cm) pieces
1 cup (160 g) potato starch
½ cup (64 g) sesame seeds
Oil, for deep-frying
Lemon wedges, for garnish

MARINADE
3 tablespoons soy sauce
2 cloves garlic, grated
1½ tablespoons sugar
1 tablespoon saké
1 tablespoon rice wine vinegar
1 tablespoon ginger juice (see "Making Ginger Juice," page 15) (optional)

1. To make the Marinade, shake together the ingredients in a large, resealable plastic bag until the sugar has dissolved.

2. Add the chicken and toss until evenly coated.

3. Let marinate in the refrigerator (tossing occasionally) 2 hours to overnight. Remove the chicken from the marinade and discard the liquid.

4. Combine the potato starch and sesame seeds in a large shallow bowl or resealable plastic bag. Lightly coat the chicken in the potato starch mixture and let rest on a wire rack until dry, about 20 minutes.

5. Meanwhile, in a deep-fryer, stockpot or large wok, heat 2 inches (5 cm) of oil to 360°F (180°C).

6. Fry the chicken, a few pieces at a time, until they float to the top and turn deep golden brown, 3 to 5 minutes. Using a slotted spoon or chopsticks, carefully remove the chicken and let drain on a clean wire rack. Repeat with the remaining chicken pieces.

7. The chicken is ready to eat now. Or, if you wish to create an extra-crispy (and delicious!) coating, increase the oil temperature to 375°F (190°C) and fry the chicken pieces a *second* time. Return the fried chicken pieces to the hotter oil and fry, in batches, an additional 2 to 3 minutes. Using a slotted spoon or chopsticks, carefully remove the chicken and let drain on a clean wire rack. Repeat with the remaining chicken pieces.

8. Garnish with lemon wedges, encouraging guests to squeeze some of the juice over the chicken before eating, if desired.

Cooking Tips *Any cut of chicken will work for this recipe, but for the best flavor, use boneless chicken thighs with the skin still on.*

See "Deep-Frying 101" on page 17 for more tips.

Soy-Glazed Chicken Wings

I swear I originally learned this dish from my friend Atsuko—but she insists she's never made it. Either way, these chicken wings are a super-quick dish that is perfect for a weeknight meal (I like to marinate the wings before leaving for work in the morning). Or, serve as an appetizer at your next party.

SERVES 4

2 lbs (1 kg) chicken wings, tips removed, drumettes & wings separated (see "Preparing Chicken Wings" on this page)

MARINADE
¼ cup (65 ml) soy sauce
2 tablespoons grated garlic, or to taste
2 tablespoons grated ginger, or to taste
2 tablespoons saké
2 tablespoons sugar

1. To make the Marinade, shake together the ingredients in a large resealable plastic bag until the sugar is dissolved.

2. Add the prepared wings and drumettes, refrigerate, and marinate for half a day to overnight, tossing occasionally.

3. Bring the chicken to room temperature, about 15 minutes.

4. Turn the broiler to high and set the oven rack 3 to 5 inches (7.5 to 12.75 cm) from the heat source.

5. Place the marinated chicken wings and drumettes on an aluminum foil–lined sheet pan. Broil until cooked through and the skin is crisp and browned, but not burnt, about 10 minutes—no need to flip the wings. (Depending on the size and shape of your broiler, you may need to rotate the sheet pan halfway through cooking for even browning.)

Cooking Tip *If your oven does not have a broiler, roast the wings on a cooling rack placed over an aluminum foil–lined baking sheet at 450°F (230°C) for 18 minutes, or until they turn a deep caramel color. Using this method, though, the skin won't get quite as deliciously crispy as if cooked under the broiler.*

Preparing Chicken Wings

1. With a chef's knife, cut off the wing tip and discard.

2. Cut into the skin between the 2 larger sections of the wing until you hit the joint. Bend back the two sections to pop and break the joint.

3. Cut through the skin and flesh to completely separate the 2 meaty portions. Repeat with the rest of the chicken wings.

Soy-Glazed Chicken Wings

Ginger-Simmered Chicken Chikuzenni/Gameni

Although *Chikuzenni* is the formal, common name, *Gameni* is how it's known in the local dialect, and how Shizuka, who taught me how to make this dish, refers to it.

SERVES 4 TO 6

One 2-in (5-cm) piece fresh ginger root, peeled and sliced into thin rounds, peel reserved

1 cup (60 g) snow peas

1 cup (170 g) peeled and chopped carrot (from about 1 carrot)

1 cup (190 g) peeled and chopped taro root or potato (from about 3 taro root or small potatoes)

1 cup (120 g) lotus root, peeled and cut into half moons, or water chestnuts

1 cup (250 ml) soy sauce

½ cup (125 ml) saké

¼ cup (50 g) sugar

¼ cup (65 ml) mirin

4 boneless, skinless chicken thighs (about 1 lb/500g), cut into 1-in (2.5-cm) pieces

1 cup (100 g) reconstituted, stemmed, and thinly sliced shiitake mushrooms (from about 10 dried)

Fresh ginger, peeled and thinly sliced lengthwise (from about a 2-in/5-cm piece), for garnish

1 recipe White Rice (page 28)

Cooking Tips Chikuzenni *is best served in winter when the vegetables called for are at their peak.*

The lotus root will quickly discolor after being cut. To prevent this from happening, place in a small bowl of water with a tablespoon or two of lemon juice or white vinegar until ready to use.

If unable to find taro root, use small waxy, red-skinned potatoes instead.

1. Bring a large pot of lightly salted water and the reserved ginger peel to a boil. Add the snow peas and blanch for 30 seconds. Remove the peas with a slotted spoon and immediately plunge into ice water to cool. Drain and set aside.

2. In the same pot of boiling water with the ginger peel, blanch the carrot and taro root together for 5 minutes. Remove with a slotted spoon. Set aside.

3. Blanch the lotus root for 2 minutes in the same pot. Remove with a slotted spoon and set aside. Discard the water and ginger peel.

4. In the same pot used to blanch the vegetables (the pot should now be empty), bring the soy sauce, saké, sugar, mirin and sliced ginger rounds just to a boil. Add the chicken, reduce the heat to medium-low and simmer for 5 minutes, or until cooked through. Using a slotted spoon, remove the chicken and set aside.

5. Add the reconstituted shiitake and the blanched carrot, taro root and lotus root to the soy sauce mixture. Simmer until most of the liquid has been absorbed and the vegetables are tender, 5 to 10 minutes. Add the chicken and blanched snow peas and stir to combine.

6. Place in a shallow serving dish and garnish with the thinly sliced ginger. Serve with rice.

Yakitori Chicken Skewers

Yakitori is found throughout Japan, most commonly at street festivals, *izakaya* (pubs that serve food), food stalls, and the grab 'n go section of the local supermarket. I made many a stop at the neighborhood yakitori stand for a quick, cheap dinner on my way home from teaching. And when my friend finally arrived in Iwaki after a long day of travel from the United States, it was off to an izakaya for skewer upon skewer of yakitori that we headed. While yakitori is not typically made at home, it is actually a very easy dish to prepare. Simply put, yakitori is broiled or grilled chicken skewers with a sweet basting sauce. It is the sauce that makes yakitori so delicious. You can either brush on the sauce or, to mimic the traditional method, dip the skewers directly into it. If dipping, do as Masako Yamaoka suggests in her book, *A First Book of Japanese Cooking*: Pour the sauce into a wide-mouthed jar (or tall, narrow glass) of adequate depth to allow the entire skewer to be completely submerged. Yakitori is best served piping hot straight off the grill. Fortunately, all the "parts" of the recipe (the sauce, chicken and green onion preparation) can be done ahead of time.

Yakitori Chicken Skewers

MAKES 9 SKEWERS

1 lb (500 g) boneless, skinless chicken thighs, cut into 1½-in (3.75-cm) lengths

18 green onions (scallions), white parts only, cut into 1½-in (3.75-cm) lengths

Flavorful Yakitori Sauce (see opposite page), at room temperature

Lemon wedges, for garnish (optional)

Shichimi togarashi or ground red pepper (cayenne), for garnish (optional)

1. Skewer 3 pieces of chicken onto a pre-soaked bamboo skewer, alternating with 2 pieces of green onion, starting and ending with a piece of chicken. (So, you should have chicken–onion–chicken–onion–chicken).

2. Turn the broiler to high and set the oven rack 3 to 5 inches (7.5 to 12.75 cm) from the heat source.

3. On an aluminum foil–lined sheet pan, broil the skewers for 3 minutes. Flip, and broil for another 2 minutes. (Use tongs or an oven mitt to protect your hands; the skewers are hot!) The chicken should now be almost, but not completely, cooked. Baste the skewers with the Yakitori Sauce (or dip as described above), and broil for 2 more minutes, or until cooked through. Baste or dip again and broil once more briefly.

4. Serve with lemon wedges and *shichimi togarashi*, if desired.

Cooking Tips *This recipe can be prepared on a grill or in a broiler. As most kitchen ovens have a broiler, I have provided specific instructions for broiling the chicken skewers. (Note: When broiling, the extra sauce will bubble and burn on the sheet pan, so be sure to line with aluminum foil.) If you'd like to use a grill, set up the grill for direct grilling, clean and oil the grates and preheat to high. Use the cooking times provided as a guideline, not a rule, as the temperature of the grill/broiler, and size of the chicken pieces, can vary greatly.*

Special Equipment *Bamboo skewers soaked in water for 30 minutes; basting brush*

Flavorful Yakitori Sauce

To replicate the depth of flavor in traditional *yakitori* sauce, where the skewers are dipped repeatedly into the sauce, Shizuo Tsuji, in his classic Japanese cookbook, *Japanese Cooking: A Simple Art*, recommends simmering a chicken bone in the sauce. In this recipe, I have suggested chicken wings instead, as Hiroko Shimbo does in her book, *The Japanese Kitchen*, because they are often easier to come by. Note: The sauce takes about an hour and a half to make, so plan accordingly. This shouldn't be too inconvenient, though, as the sauce can be made up to one month ahead of time. If you're using refrigerated sauce, bring to room temperature before basting the skewers.

MAKES 2 CUPS (500 ML)

4 chicken wings
2 cups (500 ml) soy sauce
1¼ cups (425 ml) saké
²/₃ cup (142 g) sugar
½ cup (125 ml) mirin

1. Turn the broiler to high and set the oven rack 3 to 5 inches (7.5 to 12.75 cm) from the heat source.

2. Place the chicken wings on an aluminum foil–lined sheet pan and broil until charred but not burnt, about 15 minutes, rotating the sheet pan halfway through cooking. Set aside.

3. Bring the soy sauce, saké, sugar and mirin to a boil in a medium saucepan, stirring to dissolve the sugar. Add the broiled chicken wings, reduce the heat to low, and simmer, covered, for 30 minutes. Remove the cover and continue simmering for an additional 30 minutes, or until the sauce is reduced and slightly thickened.

4. Off heat, remove the chicken wings with tongs or a slotted spoon (save for another use, or enjoy as a fun snack!). Let the sauce cool to room temperature, then strain through a paper towel– or coffee filter–lined fine-mesh sieve to remove the residual oil from the wings.

5. Store in an airtight container and refrigerate for up to 1 month.

Cooking Tip *If, when making Yakitori, you've chosen to dip the broiled chicken skewers directly into the sauce (as opposed to basting), bring any leftover sauce to a boil and then cool to room temperature before returning to the refrigerator to save for future use. This helps eliminate the residual moisture from the hot skewers along with any bacteria from the uncooked chicken, which can cause the sauce to spoil prematurely.*

Chicken and Vegetable Hotpot
Hakata Mizutaki

After a long day of traveling and confusing train schedule changes, this was the first meal I ate when I finally arrived at Michiko's warm and inviting home just outside of Fukuoka on the southern "island" of Kyushu. With tender chicken, healthy vegetables and a bright citrus dipping sauce (*ponzu*), I couldn't have hoped for anything more satisfying.

"Hakata" is the old name for this region, so many of the local dishes bear this name as a prefix. Traditionally, this cold-weather dish is made in a large earthenware *nabe* pot, complete with its own portable burner and set in the middle of the table so that refills are within easy reach.

SERVES 6

8 cups (2 liters) water

4 boneless, skinless chicken thighs, cut into 1-in (2.5-cm) pieces

1 cup (80 g) thoroughly rinsed and thinly sliced leek

3½ oz (100 g) fresh shiitake mushrooms, stemmed, with an "X" scored on top of the cap (about 1 cup)

1 package (about 3½ oz/100 g) fresh enoki mushrooms, ends trimmed and separated

4 oz (125 g) fresh eringi mushrooms, ends trimmed and thinly sliced lengthwise (about 1 cup)

4 cups (200 g) shredded Napa cabbage (about ½ cabbage)

2 cups (54 g) very thinly sliced chrysanthemum leaves (shungiku) or spinach

Green onions (scallions), trimmed and sliced

PONZU SAUCE

4 tablespoons soy sauce

3 tablespoons rice wine vinegar

3 tablespoons fresh sudachi, yuzu or lemon juice, or other available citrus

1. To make the Ponzu Sauce, combine the ingredients in a small bowl. Set aside.

2. Bring the water to a boil in a large *nabe* or stockpot. Add the chicken and simmer over medium heat for 5 minutes.

3. Add the leek and mushrooms. Simmer 5 minutes more. Off heat, add the cabbage and chrysanthemum leaves.

4. To serve, let each person pour a generous amount of the Ponzu Sauce into his or her own shallow bowl. Add a heaping spoonful of the sliced green onions to each bowl. Then, ladle in some of the chicken and veggies from the pot, letting most of the broth drain off back into the pot.

Cooking Tips *To create the best-tasting broth and most tender meat, Shizuka, Michiko's mother, recommends simmering a whole chicken in water over low heat; a delicious, albeit time-consuming option. In the recipe provided on this page, I offer a more streamlined process.*

Fresh chrysanthemum leaves (shungiku) are known for their strong herbal aroma and distinct flavor. Heat only lightly to preserve these traits. Look for shungiku at larger Japanese, Chinese and some Vietnamese markets.

Feel free to use whatever assortment of mushrooms you have on hand, and according to what your taste buds prefer.

A Note About Ponzu

The highlight of this dish is the Ponzu Sauce (soy sauce with citrus overtones). The type of citrus juice used varies depending on the season. Lemon, since it's available year round, is a reliable option. Yuzu, the coveted sour-sweet citrus unique to Japan, is available from fall to early winter. And kabosu, a very sour citrus with a thick green skin grown in Oita prefecture in southern Kyushu, is available from early fall to winter.

For a sweeter version of Ponzu Sauce than the one provided in this recipe, combine 1 tablespoon mirin, 2 tablespoons rice wine vinegar and 3 tablespoons soy sauce, plus the juice of 1 citrus, or to taste.

Mixed Japanese BBQ

It was a beautiful June evening, and Takako, Hitomi's mother, wanted to have a BBQ. Their new house boasts a spacious backyard (complete with deck) and Hitomi's dad, Toyozou, enthusiastically accepted the role of grill-meister.

And grill he did! Beef (straight out of the grocery store packaging and onto the grill, yet it was some of the most flavorful and tender meat I've ever tasted!); scallops-on-the-half shell; large, puffy squares of tofu—crisp and smoky on the outside, still soft and warm in the middle; sweet potatoes, green peppers, onions, shiitakes . . .

But what stole the show was the dipping sauce. A little sweet, a little sesame-y and with a little bit of a kick, it quickly became the reason to keep on grilling. Takako laughed when I insisted on getting the recipe, most likely because she had to reveal her "secret." She just combined two different bottles of purchased sauce, and then doctored it up a bit by adding extra grated onion.

This homemade recipe tastes even better, and you don't have to worry about scouring the shelves of your local Asian market to "make" it.

Suggested Grilling Times

• *Sweet Potato Rounds—5 to 7 minutes per side*

• *Onions—4 to 8 minutes per side*

• *Tofu—4 to 6 minutes per side*

• *Peppers—4 to 6 minutes per side*

• *Shiitake—3 to 5 minutes per side*

• *Scallops—2 to 3 minutes per side, or just until firm and opaque*

• *Beef—1 to 3 minutes per side, or to desired doneness*

SERVES 4 TO 6

8 large sea scallops, seasoned with salt and pepper

8 large fresh shiitake mushrooms, stems removed

1 block (about 1 lb/500 g) extra-firm tofu, pressed dry (see page 17) and sliced crosswise into ¾-in (2-cm) pieces

2 onions, peeled and sliced into ½-in (1.25-cm) rounds

2 green bell peppers, seeded and quartered

1½ lbs (750 g) center-cut beef tenderloin or sirloin, thinly sliced (no more than ¼-in/6-mm thick), seasoned with salt and pepper

1 large sweet potato, sliced into ¼-in (6-mm) rounds

Oil, for coating the grill

JAPANESE BBQ SAUCE

1 cup (250 ml) soy sauce

4 tablespoons sugar

2 tablespoons apple cider vinegar

2 tablespoons fresh-squeezed lemon juice (from about 1 lemon)

1 tablespoon toasted sesame seeds (see "Toasting Sesame Seeds," page 16)

1 teaspoon sesame oil

½ teaspoon shichimi togarashi, or ¼ teaspoon ground red pepper (cayenne), or to taste

½ apple, peeled, cored, and grated

½ onion, peeled and grated

1 clove garlic, grated

One 1-in (2.5-cm) piece fresh ginger, peeled and grated

1. To make the Japanese BBQ Sauce, combine all the ingredients for the sauce in a small bowl. Whisk until the sugar is dissolved. Set aside.

2. Set up the grill for direct grilling and preheat to medium-high. Grill the desired items on clean, well-oiled grates. (Tofu is especially prone to sticking.) There is no set cooking order, though if you want all of the food you're grilling to be ready at the same time, place the longest-grilling foods on first and follow with the foods that require shorter grilling times. The meat is cooked to desired doneness, the scallops until just opaque. Grill the vegetables until they are well browned, if not a little charred. See "Suggested Grilling Times" sidebar, right.

3. To serve, eat as the food comes straight off the grill, dipping into the Japanese BBQ Sauce between bites.

Cooking Tips *We prepared the barbeque with the* karubi *cut of* wagyu *beef, which comes from the lower belly of the cow. A Korean name, karubi is one of the most popular cuts served at yakiniku (grilled meat) restaurants in Japan. If you have access to this cut, by all means use it!*

If the grill grates are especially large, or the vegetables especially small, skewer the vegetables on presoaked bamboo skewers before grilling. For easier handling, wrap the ends of the skewers in aluminum foil.

If you don't have a grill, use a 400°F (200°C) electric griddle or skillet. A cast-iron grill pan would also work.

Special Equipment *Charcoal or gas grill; bamboo skewers, if using, soaked in water for 30 minutes*

Braised Spare Ribs Tonkotsu

Needing a break from the hustle and bustle of Kagoshima city, I hopped on the next train for Ibusuki, a small spa town on the southern tip of Kyushu. Once there, the first place I headed for was Satsuma-aji, a small, friendly restaurant specializing in *kyodo-ryori* (local specialties). (Throughout Kagoshima there are many references to "Satsuma" because that is what the region used to be known as.) Arriving after the lunch-hour rush, there was plenty of room for me at the counter, perched directly in front of the chef. Fortunately for me, he was eager to chat and generously shared his secret to creating these fall-off-the-bone, melt-in-your-mouth tender spare ribs.

SERVES 4

½ cup (125 ml) soy sauce, preferably light

¼ cup (65 ml) saké

3 tablespoons sugar, preferably natural cane

2 teaspoons oil

2 lbs (1 kg) pork spare ribs, divided into individual ribs

2 to 3 green onions (scallions), thinly sliced, green parts only

1 recipe White Rice (page 28)

1. Preheat the oven to 325°F (160°C).

2. Whisk together the soy sauce, saké and sugar in a small bowl. Set aside.

3. Heat the oil in a large oven-proof skillet over medium-high heat. Brown the spare ribs, in batches, until they easily release from the pan and have a good crust, about 3 minutes per side. Remove from the skillet, repeat with the remaining spare ribs, and set aside.

4. Pour in the soy sauce mixture (careful, it may bubble vigorously), return the spare ribs to the skillet, and bring just to a boil (this will happen very quickly).

5. Cover, and braise in the oven for 2 hours (flipping after 1 hour, and then again after another half hour), or until the meat easily separates from the bone.

6. Garnish with the green onions. Serve with hot rice and any remaining sauce. (Before serving, you may prefer to skim off the layer of oil floating on top of the sauce.)

Variation: Braised Pork Shoulder

You can also make this recipe with 2 lbs (1 kg) bone-in pork shoulder. Sear one side of the meat in 2 teaspoons of oil until browned (about 3 minutes), then flip, add the soy sauce mixture, bring to a boil. Cover and braise in the oven until the meat easily separates from the bone, about 2½ hours. Flip the meat while braising after every hour.

Cooking Tip *If you ask nicely, your butcher will divide the spare ribs into individual ribs for you.*

Special Equipment *Oven-proof skillet with 2½-inch (6.25-cm) sides, or a Dutch oven, with cover*

Braised Spare Ribs

CURRY RICE Kare Raisu

Curry Rice is a fast, cheap, delicious staple that is enjoyed by children, college students, families, salary men . . . everyone. The dish is made in homes, enjoyed at restaurants, or wolfed down at curry shops, where you order from a machine outside, present your ticket inside, and quickly eat your meal in the brightly lit dinerlike setting. While each chef has his own variation—two of my favorites are *Chand Mera* in Tabito and *Graphity* in Iwaki—the base of most home-cooked Japanese curry is a roux, not curry powder. Compared to its Indian counterpart, Japanese curry is much sweeter. To help balance the sweetness, use Amy Kaneko's tip from her book, *Let's Cook Japanese Food!*, of adding both soy sauce and Worcestershire sauce.

This recipe yields a lot of Curry Rice, which is intentional. It freezes and reheats well, making it the perfect dish to prepare one winter Sunday afternoon, portioning it into small containers for weekday meals.

SERVES 6+

2 tablespoons butter

1 tablespoon oil

1 lb (500 g) boneless pork shoulder, cut into 1-in (2.5-cm)-chunks, seasoned with salt and pepper

2 large onions, thinly sliced

3 cloves garlic, minced

One 1-in (2.5-cm) knob fresh ginger root, peeled and minced

4 cups (1 liter) chicken stock

4 carrots, peeled and roughly chopped

2 potatoes, peeled and roughly chopped

4¼ oz (135 g) mild, medium or hot Japanese curry roux (½ packet), broken into smaller pieces

2 tablespoons soy sauce (optional)

2 tablespoons Worcestershire sauce (optional)

1 recipe White Rice (page 28)

Red pickled ginger slivers (beni shoga)

1. Heat the butter and oil in a large stockpot over medium-high heat. Add half of the pork shoulder and cook until browned on all sides, about 5 minutes. Remove with a slotted spoon and repeat with the remaining pork. Set aside.

2. Lower the heat to medium, add the onions, scraping up the brown bits on the bottom of the pan with a wooden spoon, and cook until translucent and starting to caramelize, 10 to 15 minutes. Add the garlic and ginger and cook until fragrant, about 1 minute more.

3. Return the meat and residual juices to the pan, pour in the chicken stock and bring to a boil. Reduce the heat to low, cover, and simmer, stirring occasionally, for 1½ hours.

4. Add the chopped carrots and potatoes, cover, and cook until fork-tender, about 30 minutes.

5. Add the roux and stir until dissolved. Simmer, stirring constantly so as not to burn the bottom, 5 minutes more. Off heat, taste the curry and, if it is too sweet for your liking, stir in the optional soy sauce and Worcestershire sauce. Serve with rice and pickled ginger.

Cooking Tips *Curry roux is available in larger grocery stores and Asian markets. It comes in scored bars that resemble chocolate (be sure to buy the roux, also called "sauce mix," not the premade sauce sold in similar boxes). In the United States, House and S&B's Golden Curry are popular brands.*

This recipe calls for pork shoulder, but if you're short on time a faster-cooking cut of pork—or beef—may be substituted.

Breaded Pork Cutlets
Tonkatsu

*T*onkatsu is a very inexpensive homestyle dish. While frequently made at home, Tonkatsu is also a popular offering at many family-friendly restaurants throughout Japan, where it's served as a set meal comprised of breaded, fried pork cutlets, shredded cabbage, white rice, miso soup and a small side of pickles. For a simpler meal, I like to serve Tonkatsu with just two sides: shredded cabbage tossed with Sesame Salad Dressing (page 35) and the requisite White Rice (page 28).

For as many people who prepare Tonkatsu, there are just as many varieties—especially with the sauce. In Nagoya, *misokatsu* is the specialty, the fried pork served with a miso-based sauce. And at *Bistro Bordeaux* in Nagasaki, I found what may be the most unique variation out there: Turkey Rice (named after the country, not the poultry). The dish consists of Tonkatsu, served on a bed of rice pilaf, with a side of spaghetti . . . all on the same plate! The dish has gained an almost cultlike following, especially among the younger generation who favor it more for its quantity than quality.

SERVES 4 TO 6

½ head cabbage (about 1 lb/500 g)

Six ½-in (1.25-cm)-thick boneless pork loin chops (4 to 6 oz/125 to 175 g each)

Salt and freshly ground black pepper, for seasoning

All-purpose flour, for coating

3 eggs, beaten

Panko (Japanese bread crumbs), for coating

Oil, for deep-frying

Prepared hot mustard (Japanese, Chinese or Colman's)

Lemon wedges

Sesame Salad Dressing (page 35)

TONKATSU SAUCE

4 tablespoons ketchup

2 tablespoons Worcestershire sauce

1 tablespoon soy sauce

2 teaspoons prepared hot mustard (Japanese, Chinese or Colman's)

¼ teaspoon freshly ground black pepper

1. To make the Tonkatsu Sauce, whisk together the ingredients in a small bowl. Set aside.

2. Finely shred the cabbage. (For best results, use a mandoline slicer or *benriner*, a Japanese mandoline slicer.) Set aside.

3. Place a pork loin chop between two layers of plastic wrap and pound until about half as thick and twice as wide. (To pound the meat, you can use the smooth side of a meat tenderizer, the bottom of a drinking glass, or the side of a large chef's knife or cleaver.) Score the edges of the chop, cutting through the fat rim, to prevent the meat from curling when fried. Season both sides with salt and pepper. Repeat with the remaining chops.

4. Heat 2 inches (5 cm) of oil in a deep-fryer, stockpot or large wok to 350°F (175°C).

5. Meanwhile, coat the seasoned pork chop with flour, shaking off any excess. Dip the chop into the eggs, and then dredge in the *panko*. Place on a wire rack and repeat with the remaining chops.

6. Deep-fry the chops in batches of one or two—so as not to crowd the pan—until deep golden brown and cooked through, about 5 minutes. Place on a wire rack to drain and repeat with the remaining chops.

7. If serving the meal with chopsticks, slice the fried pork crosswise into ¾-inch (2-cm) pieces. Otherwise, the chops can be served whole.

8. Serve with a large mound of the shredded cabbage, a lemon wedge and dollop of spicy mustard placed on the edge of the plate. The Tonkatsu Sauce can either be poured directly over the meat, or used as a dipping sauce. Provide Sesame Salad Dressing for drizzling over the shredded cabbage.

Cooking Tips *If you're pressed for time, look for bottled Bull Dog sauce. It's a convenient substitute for homemade Tonkatsu Sauce. (The brand is as synonymous with Tonkatsu as A-1 is to steak in the United States.)*

The Tonkatsu Sauce can easily be doubled. (It's a great all-purpose dipping sauce and will keep for up to 1 month in the refrigerator.)

See "Deep-Frying 101" on page 17 for more tips.

Special Equipment *Mandoline slicer or benriner, a Japanese mandoline slicer*

Sesame-Seared Beef

This dish is traditionally served with a miniature grill or electric hot plate set in the middle of the table and a small block of suet provided to grease the surface. Diners then grill their meat and vegetables as they eat—hot off the grill and straight into their mouths.

As the prep time for this dish is minimal, and the marinade comes together in just minutes, this is the perfect dish to throw together before work in the morning. You'll have dinner ready within twenty minutes of getting home (the time it takes to cook the rice).

And as one recipe tester pointed out, with the traditional vegetable and rice accompaniments, this dish is a good representation of how to feed four people with just one pound of meat.

SERVES 4

1 lb (500 g) well-marbled beef sirloin, cut against the grain into ⅛ to ¼-in (3 to 6-mm)-thick slices, then—depending on the size of the slices—cut again into large bite-sized pieces

1 onion, cut into large segments

1 green pepper, cut into large slices

Oil

1 recipe White Rice (page 28)

MARINADE

5 tablespoons soy sauce

3 tablespoons sugar

2 tablespoons ground toasted sesame seeds (see "Toasting Sesame Seeds," page 16)

2 tablespoons grated onion

1 tablespoon saké

1 tablespoon sesame oil

½ teaspoon fresh ground black pepper

1. To make the Marinade, combine the ingredients in a large resealable plastic bag. Seal the bag and shake to dissolve the sugar.

2. Add the beef, onion and green pepper and marinate in the refrigerator for half a day to overnight, tossing occasionally.

3. Prior to cooking, remove the bag from the refrigerator and bring the ingredients to room temperature. Separate the meat from the veggies and discard the Marinade.

4. Meanwhile, heat a well-seasoned cast-iron skillet or flat-surfaced griddle over high heat until very hot. Add just enough oil to coat the surface (about 1 tablespoon). Add the onion and green pepper and cook, stirring often, until blistered and lightly charred, about 5 minutes. Remove from the skillet.

5. Add more oil if necessary—just enough to maintain a light coating.

6. Add a few pieces of meat to the pan, so as not to crowd, and cook undisturbed until well seared, flipping once, 30 to 45 seconds per side for medium doneness. Repeat with the remaining meat. (For a better sear on the second side, flip and place on a previously open area of the pan where the temperature will be higher. Serve immediately with rice.

Cooking Tip *Sirloin can be a tough cut of meat. For this reason, be sure the cuts are small enough to fit in your mouth in one bite. A large piece of sirloin will be difficult to eat if dining with chopsticks.*

Special Equipment *Well-seasoned cast-iron skillet or flat-surfaced griddle*

CHAPTER 5

Seafood

When most people think of Japanese food, sushi is what comes to mind. And they'd be right. The dish is a mainstay. You can enjoy sushi at high-class establishments where the meal will cost hundreds of dollars; or, pop in for *kaiten sushi* where the pieces come floating by on a conveyor belt, and you're charged by the number and color of empty plates stacked in front of you. Even easier, pick up a box of pre-made sushi at the train station or grab 'n go section of the grocery store on your way home from work.

But being a small country surrounded by water, it's only natural that Japanese seafood dishes go way beyond sushi. The collection of recipes in this chapter are some of my favorites.

Of course, the main thing to remember when preparing any fish dish is to use the freshest fish available. Sometimes that means substituting the type of fish called for in the recipe. And know that this is okay— actually encouraged. Most, if not all, of the recipes in this chapter work well with other varieties of fish. So get creative and have fun preparing these dishes with whatever fish seems to be calling your name!

Seasoned Fish Burgers
Sanma Po Po Yaki

An oily fish, *sanma* (pacific saury) is a local specialty of the seaside town of Onahama, and its low cost makes it especially popular with home cooks. So popular, in fact, that when I was headed to Tokyo for an important business meeting, it was suggested I present a cooler-full of fresh sanma to the host.

Sanma Po Po Yaki is a classic recipe for the fish. The mixture can either be formed into large, thin patties and then fried (functioning as a bun-less burger), or rolled into small, thick "fishballs" which are then simmered in soup.

Sanma is known to have a "fishy" smell to it. But the strong aromatics in this recipe (leek, *shiso*, ginger) counteract it perfectly.

A bit on the spicy side, Sanma Po Po Yaki is considered a *saké-ate*—a great accompaniment to saké and beer. Try serving these seasoned fish burgers with the Wasabi Mayo (page 119) or Ginger Mayo (page 122).

MAKES 6 SMALL BURGERS

1 cup (100 g) thoroughly cleaned and coarsely chopped leek

2 shiso or 4 basil leaves, thinly sliced

One 1½-in (3.75-cm) piece ginger, peeled and grated

1 teaspoon salt

¾ teaspoon shichimi togarashi or ¼ teaspoon ground red pepper (cayenne), or to taste

1 lb (500 g) Pacific Saury (sanma) fillets, with skin on, or other fatty fish fillets, skinned, and cut into 1-in (2.5-cm) chunks

1 tablespoon oil, plus more as needed

6 lemon wedges

Double recipe Wasabi Mayo (page 119) or Ginger Mayo (page 122) (optional)

1. Combine the leek, shiso, ginger, salt and *shichimi togarashi* in a food processor. Process just until finely chopped. Add the fish fillets and pulse 4 to 5 more times, or just until the fish is coarsely chopped and the mixture is well combined and just starting to stick together. (For best texture, be careful not to over-process the fish.)

2. Using ¼-cup (65-ml) measure, shape the mixture into 6 burgers; flatten slightly and place on a large plate. Cover and refrigerate 30 minutes, or until firm.

3. Heat 1 tablespoon of oil in a large skillet over medium-low heat. When hot, add enough burgers so as not to crowd and fry until browned and cooked through, about 3 minutes per side. Repeat with the remaining burgers, adding more oil if necessary.

4. Squeeze a lemon wedge over each burger before serving. If desired, serve with Wasabi Mayo or Ginger Mayo on the side.

Cooking Tip Sanma *(pacific saury or mackerel pike) is a long, sleek fish with a silver-blue sparkle. It's considered a fall fish because that is when it has obtained its highest fat content. If unavailable, try another fatty fish, like mackerel, tuna, or swordfish.*

Special Equipment *Food processor*

Scallops with Miso and Eggs
Kaiyaki Miso

Kaiyaki Miso is a reason to head straight for Aomori prefecture. Taking advantage of its proximity to Mutsu Bay, this local cuisine is a prime example of northern Japanese comfort food. Anywhere I'd go while traveling the area, I'd ask about this dish, and, guaranteed, every time I'd get an excited, high-pitched squealing reply of "*OISHI!*" ("Delicious!"). Everyone seemed to love Kaiyaki Miso and wanted to share their personal anecdote about it. My favorite was the sixty-plus-year-old woman who told me of regularly eating the dish while breastfeeding her children. When recounting the tale, she kept repeatedly and exaggeratingly clutching her breasts, all the while laughing and drawing attention to herself, visibly enjoying the memories evoked by her light-hearted storytelling.

While waiting to catch the limited-route bus to the remote hostel where I was staying on yet another gloomy, rainy night, I headed to the nearby Rokubei *izakaya* (bar that serves food) for shelter. I had heard this was *the* place to try Kaiyaki Miso (it's a dish that's mainly eaten at home, which made sampling the specialty difficult for visitors like myself), and I ended up helping myself to two(!) orders. The second time around, the chef graciously walked me through the process.

I learned that even at the source, scallops are expensive. To make a little go a long way, the scallops are chopped up into smaller pieces and then combined with egg and leek. When I ate this dish in Japan, it was prepared in half of a scallop shell over an open flame. Cooking it this way is said to impart a strong "sea" flavor. And it *was* delicious. But also a bit impractical as real scallop shells are hard to come by. Open-flame cooking is also dangerous without practice, and not all of us even have a gas stove.

The method provided here still produces tasty results without a lot of fuss. At the izakaya, *aji-no-moto* (MSG) was sprinkled over the eggs just before serving. I substitute with salt and find it does an equally good job of making the flavors "pop." For everyday meals, a small bowl or plate works just fine for serving Kaiyaki Miso. But for a more formal presentation, try serving it in porcelain shell-shaped dishes to emulate the natural scallop shell the dish is traditionally prepared in. One final note: If you ever have a chance to visit the food market at the Auga Building in the port city of Aomori, go. It sells some of the freshest, most beautiful seafood I've ever seen. With exotic sea creatures slowly crawling their way off purchase plates, scallop shells gracefully breathing open and closed, enormous, record-breaking crabs, and neon-red roe among the bounty of offerings for sale . . . it's truly a sight to behold.

Scallops with Miso and Eggs

SERVES 4 AS A SIDE DISH

2 tablespoons finely sliced leek

2 jumbo scallops (each about 1¼ oz/35 g), each cut into 8 pieces (for a total of 16 pieces)

4 eggs, lightly beaten

Salt, to taste

MISO SAUCE

1 tablespoon water

4 teaspoons saké

2 teaspoons red or white miso (or, for a more complex flavor, use 1 teaspoon each of red and white miso)

1. To make the Miso Sauce, whisk together the ingredients in a small bowl. Set aside.
2. Add the leek, scallop and Miso Sauce in a small skillet over medium heat. When the mixture starts to bubble, add the eggs and scramble everything together until cooked through, 2 to 3 minutes more. Sprinkle with salt and serve.

Broiled Salmon
Shiojake

This version of salmon is saltier and drier than you may be used to—but no less delicious! It is typically served for breakfast with rice, pickles, *umeboshi* (pickled Japanese apricots), miso soup, toasted nori sheets and green tea.

It can also be flaked into smaller pieces and used as a filling for Almond Rice Onigiri (page 72)—or to top a pasta or salad. Because of the simplicity of this dish, it's best to use the freshest, highest-quality salmon available.

SERVES 4

4 center-cut salmon fillets, skin on (about 5 to 6 oz/150 to 175 g each), preferably Sockeye or Coho
Salt, preferably sea salt (about 1 to 1½ teaspoons per fillet)
Oil
Mirin
Peeled and grated daikon
4 lemon wedges (optional)
Soy sauce (optional)

1. Liberally salt all sides of the salmon fillets
2. Place the salted fillets skin-side up on a rack fitted inside a sheet pan and refrigerate for 2 to 3 hours. Discard the drained liquid and pat the fillets dry with paper towels. Set aside.
3. Turn the broiler to high and set the oven rack 3 to 5 inches (7.5 to 12.75 cm) from the heat source.
4. Dry the sheet pan and line with aluminum foil; lightly coat with oil.
5. Place the salmon skin-side up on the prepared sheet pan and broil for 6 minutes, or until the skin is bubbly and browned. Flip, and broil until cooked through, about 6 minutes more.
6. Remove from the heat and lightly brush the salmon flesh with mirin, which gives it a nice sheen.
7. Serve each fillet with some grated daikon, a lemon wedge and/or soy sauce for squeezing/drizzling over, if desired.

Note *The salmon needs to rest in the refrigerator for 3 hours before broiling, so be sure to plan accordingly.*

HaNdRoLLed Sushi
Temakizushi

When it finally came time to enjoy the sushi sampler I had spent the afternoon helping prepare with my friend Ayano's family, we retreated to the one common area of the apartment—all five of us crowded around the small lacquered table in the cozy four-mat tatami room. This was family, and they immediately made me feel a part of it. Even with all the amazing food, fresh seafood, and Nobuyuki, Ayano's father, assembling sushi faster than we could possibly eat, I still couldn't keep myself away from this embarrassingly simple, do-it-yourself combination: Crisp nori loosely wrapped around tangy rice and creamy, perfectly ripe avocado before being dipped into wasabi-spiked soy sauce just before biting. Eureka, my new favorite food!

These handheld rolls are designed for experimentation. Play around with the different fillings—crab and cucumber are especially popular additions. Just don't overstuff or they'll be too difficult to eat. This is the perfect simple, communal meal to invite some friends over, sit around a table and drink beer with. It would be just as fitting served at a party in do-it-yourself buffet style.

MAKES 10 LARGE ROLLS OR 20 SMALLER ROLLS

1 recipe Sushi Rice (page 29)

5 sheets toasted nori seaweed, each cut into 2 rectangles (4 x 7½ in/10 x 19 cm) or 4 squares (about 4 x 4-in/10 x 10-cm)

1 perfectly ripe avocado, thinly sliced

8 crab sticks, cut in half lengthwise, or 6 oz (175 g) lump crab meat, picked over for shell

2 Japanese or "baby" cucumbers (or 1 small English (hothouse) cucumber), cut lengthwise into 3 x ¼-in (7.5 cm x 6-mm) strips

Shiso leaves (optional)

Chives (optional)

Pickled Ginger (page 30) (optional)

DIPPING SAUCE

Soy sauce

Wasabi paste or freshly grated wasabi, to taste

Cooking Tip *Although smaller squares of nori are available, it's usually more convenient to cut the easier-to-find larger sheets (7½ x 8 inches/19 x 20 cm) into four smaller squares.*

1. For the Dipping Sauce, provide each dining companion with a small condiment bowl. Encourage them to combine some soy sauce and a dab of wasabi, stirring them together with a fork or the tips of their chopsticks.

2. To assemble a roll, spread a thin layer of Sushi Rice over the non-shiny side of a nori rectangle or square. Top with your choice of ingredients, then gently fold the edges together as if making a taco. (To shape into a cone as shown in the photograph on opposite page, first add your fillings. Then fold one corner of the nori to the center of the square. Finish the shape by rolling the nori at an angle around the fillings.)

3. Dip in the wasabi-spiked soy sauce, if desired, and eat.

4. Serve with a small mound of Pickled Ginger, if using, eating a sliver or two between each new roll.

Sea Bream Rice Tai Meshi

After an utterly failed attempt at an informational interview on Matsuyama's local food culture earlier in the morning, I found myself walking for over an hour—weighted down with my overflowing backpack and cumbersome laptop—trying to find a restaurant that, just-my-luck, ended up being closed for lunch. I was desperate for some sort of relief from the hot streets and unrelenting sun, so on a whim, I decided to stop at EPIC (Ehime Prefectural International Centre) to pick up a free copy of the area's discount card. I mentioned to the attendant that I was interested in the area's local cuisine, and, specifically, I really wanted to learn how to make *Tai Meshi*. As word quickly spread around the office of the foreigner's strange request, the Director, quietly observing from his desk along the back wall, immediately phoned his fisherman friend, instructing him to go catch us some *tai* (sea bream). And with that whirlwind of an interaction, ten minutes later I had a cooking class scheduled for 9:00 a.m. the next morning to experience the preparation of Tai Meshi firsthand!

Right on schedule, Katsuji Shigekawa, the fisherman, walked into the EPIC office. Apart from the cooler full of freshly caught fish he was carrying, he was nothing like I expected. He clearly had dressed up for the occasion. His healthy, naturally weathered face was freshly shaven. His laborer's body was unaccustomed to his sport coat, and he immediately took it off. He wore plaid slacks, later stained with fish guts from cleaning the sea bream, and thick, grey-blue socks bulging out of his worn, tasseled dress shoes. It was a big deal that he was coming to cook for a foreigner, and I felt honored that the foreigner was me.

While cleaning the fish, Katsuji used the fish's natural secretions to stick the tails to the wall. We were all laughing at this, thinking he was just trying to be funny, but actually, he corrected us, it's an old tradition: The tails were left on the wall to dry so that when bad weather hit, or fish were scarce, these dried tails could be used to make stock.

When it comes to preparing Tai Meshi, there seem to be two camps: In Uwajima, on the south-western side of Shikoku, thin slices of tai are served raw like sashimi, dipped into a mixture of soy sauce, raw egg and sesame seeds, and served with hot white rice. Just a few hours north in Matsuyama (where I was having the Tai Meshi cooking class), a whole fish is used, cooked simultaneously with the rice. At the EPIC office, two of the workers, one from the South and one from the North, were arguing, in fun, over which version was more traditional, and which tasted better. Having sampled both varieties, at least in my mind, the woman from the north had it right. Katsuji prepared this northern version of Tai Meshi, and it is his recipe listed here.

SERVES 6 AS A SIDE DISH

- 1 piece konbu kelp (about 5 x 4 in/12.75 x 10 cm)
- 1 whole sea bream (tai) or red snapper (about 1⅓ lbs/650 g), scaled and gutted, or 1⅓ lbs (650 g) sea bream or red snapper fillets
- 2¼ cups (565 ml) water
- 2 cups (440 g) uncooked short-grain white "sushi" rice, washed, and left to drain 30 minutes (see "Rice Making 101," page 28)
- 2 tablespoons soy sauce, preferably light
- 2 teaspoons instant dashi powder
- Two 3 x 5-in (7.5 x 12.75-cm) sheets fried tofu (abura-age), rolled in paper towel to remove excess oil and thinly sliced

1. To remove any dirt or grit, lightly wipe the *konbu* with a damp paper towel. (Konbu has a white powder on it, a source of a lot of konbu's flavor. Use light pressure so as not to wipe it off.) Break the konbu into 1-in (2.5-cm) strips.

2. If using a whole fish, to help release the flavors of the fish into the rice, use the tip of a sharp knife to score a large "X" into each side of the prepared sea bream taking care not to cut into the flesh itself. Set aside.

3. Add the water, washed rice, soy sauce and instant dashi powder in a large Dutch oven. Top with the sliced fried tofu and konbu. Bring to a boil over high heat. Place the whole fish (or fillets, if using) on top of the rice, cover tightly, reduce the heat to low, and cook for 35 minutes.

4. Turn off the heat and let rest (without removing the lid) for 10 minutes.

5. When you open the cover, everything will have swollen and expanded, especially the konbu, which will have become at least double in size.

6. Using chopsticks or tongs, remove the konbu as well as the bones, fins and fish head (they will easily break away).

7. Mix together the rice and fish meat and serve. Be mindful of stray bones when eating.

Cooking Tips *Katsuji made* Tai Meshi *in his 10-cup rice cooker. I've adapted the recipe to work in a Dutch oven—a more typical piece of cookware in the West. If you'd like to use a rice cooker, make sure the size of the cooker is large enough to house the fish. Cook according to the manufacturer's instructions, including the water-to-rice ratio.*

In the West, sea bream (tai) is available fresh or frozen at large Asian markets. If unavailable, red snapper may be used instead. If the idea of using a whole fish seems unsettling—or you don't have a cooking vessel large enough to accommodate it—fish fillets may be used instead.

Special Equipment *Dutch oven, ideally oval and made of clay or enameled cast iron, or a large rice cooker*

A Note About Tai

Tai is considered a healthy fish that is very low in oil. Tai is also considered a celebratory food in Japan. So much so, that a pun has evolved on the word for congratulations, omedetai. *An expensive fish (although its price varies greatly with the season), it's especially common to see tai at wedding ceremonies since the fish's beautiful peach-red color is a symbol of happiness in Japan. There are over 100 varieties of tai, but one of the best,* madai, *can be found in the Inland Sea, the waters between mainland Honshu and the large island of Shikoku.*

A Cook's Journey to Japan

One-Bite Sushi Nibbles
Temarizushi

Impressive to look at, this version of sushi is actually incredibly easy to prepare. It makes a great addition to a sushi platter or the perfect appetizer.

MAKES ABOUT 8 DOZEN BALLS

1 recipe Sushi Rice (page 29)
5 oz (150 g) smoked salmon, sliced paper thin
Chives, cut into 1-in (2.5-cm) lengths

WASABI MAYO
2 tablespoons mayonnaise
1 teaspoon wasabi paste or freshly grated wasabi, or to taste

1. To make the Wasabi Mayo, mix the mayonnaise and wasabi together in a small bowl. Set aside.

2. With damp lightly salted hands, shape the Sushi Rice into 2-teaspoon-size balls. (I found that a 2-teaspoon Oxo Cookie Scoop is ideal for portioning the rice balls.)

3. Wrap each ball with a piece of salmon—squeeze gently to refine the shape and help make the salmon stick to the rice.

4. Dollop each ball with some of the Wasabi Mayo and decorate with the chives.

Cooking Tips *Let the rice cool down just enough so that it's easy to handle. (It's best to form the balls while the rice is still warm as the steam from the just-cooked rice helps the balls stick together.)*

When shaping the balls, if the rice sticks to your hands, which it most likely will, dampen them with water.

As the recipe title suggests, this sushi is intended to be easily enjoyed in just one bite. Although you'll be tempted to go bigger, keep the rice balls small. The smaller size also provides a much tastier rice-to-salmon ratio.

For this recipe, you will need thinly sliced smoked salmon. The thinner the better—it will be easier to wrap around the sushi balls.

For better "dolloping" control, make an impromptu piping cone by placing the Wasabi Mayo in the center of a sheet of parchment and rolling the sheet up to form a cone. (See the photographs, right.)

Salmon Teriyaki

Terikayki sauce is used with a number of different fish and meats in Japan. But the most common use is with *buri* (yellowtail). If you're able to find fresh yellowtail, by all means, use it. Otherwise, the version offered below, made with the easier-to-find salmon fillets, is just as delicious. Proof in point, my dad makes this dish for my ninety-three-year-old grandmother, and she licks her plate clean!

SERVES 4

4 center-cut salmon fillets (5 to 6 oz/150 to 175 g each)
Oil

TERIYAKI SAUCE
½ cup (125 ml) soy sauce
¼ cup (65 ml) saké
2 tablespoons mirin
2 tablespoons sugar

1. To make the Teriyaki Sauce, combine the ingredients in a large resealable plastic bag. Seal the bag and shake to dissolve the sugar.

2. Add the salmon and marinate in the refrigerator for 30 minutes, tossing occasionally.

3. Preheat the oven to 500°F (260°C).

4. Bring the Teriyaki Sauce and salmon to room temperature.

5. Remove the salmon from the Teriyaki Sauce, reserving the liquid, and pat the fillets dry with paper towels.

6. In a large ovenproof skillet over medium-high heat, add just enough oil to create a light film in the pan. If necessary use a paper towel to evenly coat the pan and soak up any excess oil. When hot, add the salmon fillets, skin side up, and cook until well browned, 1 to 2 minutes.

7. Gently flip the salmon fillets over and immediately place the skillet in the preheated oven. Roast for 4 minutes, or until the fish is opaque and moist and the layers flake easily when tested with the tip of a knife or fork tine, or until desired doneness.

8. Carefully remove the skillet from the hot oven and place on the stovetop. Transfer the fish to a serving plate. Add the reserved Teriyaki Sauce to the hot skillet (it will bubble vigorously) and boil over high heat until reduced, thick, and syrupy, about 2 minutes. Spoon or brush the sauce over the salmon fillets and serve warm.

Cooking Tip *Be careful when preparing this recipe so as not to burn yourself on the skillet's handle once it has been removed from the very hot oven.*

Special Equipment *Ovenproof skillet*

Salmon Teriyaki

Miso-Marinated Grilled Fish

The marinade in this recipe is meant to replicate the flavor of *saikyo miso*, a sweet, delicate white miso often used in the Kyoto area of Japan. If you have access to this harder-to-find variety, feel free to use it.

If necessary, place a small plate on the plastic wrap to keep the fish submerged in the marinade. Or, flip the fillets halfway through marinating.

When broiling, watch closely as the sugar in the miso is quick to burn.

SERVES 4

4 fish fillets, such as black cod (sable-fish), salmon, sea bass or swordfish (5 to 6 oz/150 to 175g each), skin on

MISO MARINADE
1 cup (200 g) sugar
1 cup (250 g) white miso
½ cup (125 ml) saké
½ cup (125 ml) mirin

1. To make the Miso Marinade, whisk together the ingredients in a small bowl until completely combined.

2. Place the fish in a non-reactive baking dish (8 x 8-inch/20 x 20-cm works well) and cover with the Miso Marinade. (Do not use a large baking dish as you want the fish to be completely covered in the marinade.) Place plastic wrap directly on the surface of the fish, and then use another piece of wrap to cover the top of the dish itself. Refrigerate 3 days.

3. Line a sheet pan with aluminum foil and lightly coat with oil.

4. Turn the broiler to high and set the oven rack 3 to 5 inches (7.5 to 12.75 cm) from the heat source.

5. Scrape off the excess Miso Marinade from each fillet, but do not rinse. Discard the marinade. Place the fillets on the prepared sheet pan. Broil 4 minutes per side, or until the fillets are caramelized and cooked through.

Note *The fish needs to marinate in the refrigerator for 3 days before cooking (trust me, it's well worth the wait!), so be sure to plan accordingly.*

Squid with Edamame

Hitomi has relatives who run a rustic *ryokan* (traditional Japanese inn) in a small fishing village in northern Ibaragi prefecture. One winter, we drove there to join a banquet-size table of family members to feast on the seasonal *anko nabe*—a cold-weather stew made from the very ugly, but very delicious, angler fish—and imbibe on too much saké. Months later, Hitomi returned for another visit, and, in the Japanese custom of never allowing one's guest to leave empty-handed, she arrived back home with a generous bundle of freshly caught squid. She used them to create this simple meal of squid and *edamame* tossed with a soy sauce mayonnaise. For variation, Hitomi sometimes tosses the squid with a just-as-delicious ginger mayonnaise. This is a saltier dish, and thus a perfect excuse to serve alcohol, especially a good Japanese beer like Sapporo.

Squid with Edamame

SERVES 4 TO 6

¼ cup (65 ml) saké

1 lb (500 g) fresh or frozen (and thawed) cleaned squid, cut into rings

2 tablespoons oil

2 cups (340 g) fresh or frozen shelled edamame

SOY SAUCE MAYO

¼ cup (50 g) mayonnaise

2 teaspoons soy sauce

GINGER MAYO (alternate sauce)

¼ cup (50 g) mayonnaise

2 teaspoons cream

1 teaspoon peeled and grated ginger

½ teaspoon salt, or to taste

1. In a small bowl, whisk together the ingredients for either the Soy Sauce Mayo or Ginger Mayo. Set aside.

2. In a shallow bowl, pour the saké over the squid and let soak for 5 to 10 minutes. Drain well.

3. In a large skillet over high heat, add the oil and sauté the edamame for 3 minutes, or until desired tenderness is reached. Add the squid and continue to sauté for 1 to 2 minutes, or just until the squid loses its sheen.

4. Using a slotted spoon, immediately transfer the squid mixture to a serving bowl. Toss with either mayo and serve.

Cooking Tips *To prevent squid from turning tough, it should either be cooked for a very brief time (no more than 2 to 3 minutes) or a very long time (no less than 30 minutes). This recipe demonstrates squid's tremendous quick-cooking abilities. Soaking the squid in saké before cooking is a Japanese technique for rinsing off any fishy smell, or* nama kusai.

Ideally, both the Soy Sauce Mayo and the Ginger Mayo should be made ahead of time to allow the flavors to fully develop. You might also want to make a double batch. The Soy Sauce Mayo is great for dipping vegetables into and spreading on sandwiches. The Ginger Mayo makes the perfect dipping sauce for blanched green pea pods or sautéed eringi *mushrooms.*

Variation: Squid with Greens

In place of the edamame, you can also use 1 large bunch (about 1 lb/500 g) of dark leafy greens, such as mustard greens. Follow the recipe as directed, sautéing the chopped greens for 3 minutes, or until nicely wilted. Before tossing the greens with the flavored mayonnaise, be sure to drain off any excess liquid given off by the greens during cooking; otherwise, the sauce will become disappointingly runny and diluted.

Deep-Fried Mackerel
Saba no Namban Zuke

On the way to Etsuko's aunt's house, where we were to start preparing the evening feast, we first had to stop at Etsuko's house. There, she picked up a cooler full of long, beautiful pacific mackerel (*saba*), with their dark skin and contrasting iridescent aquamarine backs. Her uncle had caught them earlier that morning expressly for us to use in the evening meal. The bright, citrus sauce and colorful vegetables with which the fish was served made the meal one of the most memorable from all my travels in Japan. If you have difficulties finding pacific mackerel, this dish works equally well with just about any in-season full-flavored fish fillet you're in the mood for.

SERVES 4

Oil, for deep-frying

6 Pacific mackerel fillets (about 1½ lbs/750 g total), or 1½ lbs (750 g) other full-flavored, fatty fish fillets, cut in half crosswise so you have 12 pieces of fish

1 cup (160 g) potato starch

½ onion, thinly sliced

3 green onions (scallions), thinly sliced

2 carrots, peeled and cut into thin matchsticks

CITRUS SAUCE

4 tablespoons soy sauce

2 tablespoons rice wine vinegar

2 tablespoons fresh-squeezed yuzu, lime, or lemon juice

¼ teaspoon shichimi togarashi or ⅛ teaspoon ground red pepper (cayenne), or to taste

1. To make the Citrus Sauce, whisk together the ingredients in a small bowl. Set aside.

2. Heat 2 inches (5 cm) of oil to 350°F (175°C) in a deep-fryer, stockpot or large wok.

3. Meanwhile, pat the fish pieces dry with paper towels. Lightly coat the fillets with potato starch. (You will have extra starch leftover, but the larger amount called for makes for easier coating.)

4. Fry the fish in batches, so as not to crowd, until crisp and golden, about 5 minutes. Using a slotted spoon, transfer the fried fish to a rack to allow the excess oil to drain off. Repeat with the remaining fish.

5. While the last batch of fish is frying, in a medium bowl mix together the onions, green onions and carrots with the Citrus Sauce and let stand 5 minutes.

6. To serve, place three pieces of fried fish on each of the four plates and top with a heaping of the onion mixture and a spoonful or two of the Citrus Sauce. Serve warm.

Cooking Tips *A mandoline or benriner (Japanese mandoline) will help you get paper-thin onion slices. If you don't have one, slice the onions as thin as you can with a sharp knife. According to Etsuko's aunt, the onion topping is used to "erase" the fish smell.*

See "Deep-Frying 101" on page 17 for more tips.

Oboke Gorge

Saving me from having to take another train ride, Etsuko was kind enough to drive me the two hours to Oboke station, where I was to start my journey to Kochi City (see "Katsuo no Tataki" Fried Eggplant Salad recipe, page 134). The route we traveled was breathtaking! Winding its way along the top of Oboke Gorge, engulfed in lush, green mountains, the narrow road could barely assert its existence amongst the power and splendor of Nature.

CHAPTER 6

Vegetables and Tofu

Writing this cookbook was a challenge for a number of different reasons, one of which was *sansai* (wild mountain vegetables). As I traveled around the country collecting recipes, people would always want to treat me to the best they had, which usually meant whatever food was at the peak of its season. And as I did the bulk of my recipe collecting from early spring to summer, that usually meant sansai. The dishes prepared with these vegetables were always delicious, but when I would learn what was on the menu for dinner that night, it would always be bittersweet. I knew these recipes could never be replicated at home—let alone anytime outside the vegetables' brief window of seasonality. It became a bit of a private joke with myself as I unknowingly planned most of my travels heading north, following the sansai harvest. As the region I was in would just be warming up, and the vegetable's availability would just be dying down, I'd inevitably head north, where the sansai season would be starting all over again.

The recipes in this chapter are still an authentic and diverse representation of what you'll find in home kitchens throughout Japan. But instead of featuring ingredients that are only available three weeks out of the year in a remote mountain village in northern Japan, they are a collection of recipes made with everyday ingredients that home cooks enjoy year round.

Fresh Eggplant Rice Topper
Dashi

*D*ashi is commonly known as fish stock. It's used as the base for most soups and sauces and is considered the heart of Japanese cooking (see recipe, page 26). When I noticed the word being used to refer to an actual *dish*, I was of course immediately intrigued.

This version of Dashi is a type of fresh *furikake* (a mixture sprinkled over hot rice, see recipe, page 30) that Hikaru, Atsuko's husband, ate growing up in his hometown of Yamagata in northern Japan. Like most Japanese dishes, though, the type of ingredients used can vary greatly depending on the area in which it's prepared. You might, for example, find the Japanese herb s*hiso* added in some incarnations.

The eggplant for this dish is not cooked, which is always surprising to Westerners. Instead, it is finely diced into ⅛-inch (3-mm) cubes and then left to marinate in a pungent sauce that penetrates the small pieces. This Fresh Eggplant Rice Topper is often eaten in summer—when many consider it too hot to slave over a stove, let alone eat. The pungent seasonings used, especially the *myoga* and *shichimi togarashi*, are intentionally intense, meant to stimulate one's appetite during the muggy summer months. (But don't be intimidated, the neutral white rice helps tone down the topping's intensity.)

This recipe can easily be doubled or tripled depending on how many people you are serving, or how much of the Dashi you choose to top your rice with.

SERVES 4 WITH RICE

1½ teaspoons peeled and grated fresh ginger or 2 whole myoga

1 cup (95 g) unpeeled, finely diced (⅛-in/ 3-mm cubes) Japanese eggplant (about 1 medium)

1 cup (70 g) thinly sliced green onions (scallions) (about 8 whole)

3 tablespoons soy sauce

¾ teaspoon shichimi togarashi or ¼ teaspoon ground red pepper (cayenne), or to taste

1 recipe White Rice (page 28)

1. If you're using myoga, blanch it, if desired, to mellow its spicy heat, then plunge in ice water to stop the cooking and drain. Clean myoga like you would a leek (slice in half lengthwise and let water run between its leaves). Thinly slice the myoga halves lengthwise.

2. Combine the ginger or myoga, eggplant, green onions, soy sauce and shichimi togarashi in a medium bowl. Let marinate 10 minutes, or up to 1 day, before serving over hot rice.

Cooking Tips *This recipe is traditionally made with myoga, a type of ginger found in Japan (see page 21). If you are able to find it, use it as a substitute for the grated ginger. Although I prefer its somewhat biting "raw" flavor, you may want to blanch myoga (whole) before using to help mellow its sharpness.*

If using the easier-to-find ginger, it's best to use a proper ginger grater when grating (see "Useful Japanese Tools and Utensils," page 12). Otherwise, the smallest side of a Western box grater will do. Just be sure to have extra ginger on hand as you lose a lot of the ginger pulp to the box grater itself.

Hikaru's mother—from whom Atsuko learned this recipe (Atsuko had never heard of this version of Dashi before getting married!)—sprinkles aji-no-moto, or MSG, *over the dish just before serving. But Atsuko thinks it tastes just fine without, so she usually omits it, as this recipe reflects.*

Fresh Eggplant Rice Topper

Spicy Carrot and Burdock Root
Kimpira Gobo

Kimpira Gobo is a traditional use for burdock, and it's one of my favorite Japanese recipes! The best part about this recipe is that it can easily be made ahead of time since it tastes just as delicious served warm or at room temperature, and it makes a great side dish for any meal. Though not traditional, I like to use Kimpira Gobo as a filling for Vegetable-Stuffed Rolls (page 40).

SERVES 6 AS A SIDE DISH

2 tablespoons soy sauce

2 tablespoons saké

2 tablespoons mirin

1 tablespoon sugar

4 cups (360 g) shaved burdock (see "Shaving Vegetables," page 15) (from about 4 burdock)

2 tablespoons oil

2 cups (200 g) peeled and shaved carrot (see "Shaving Vegetables," page 15) (from about 2 large carrots)

1 tablespoon toasted sesame seeds (see "Toasting Sesame Seeds," page 16)

½ teaspoon shichimi togarashi or ¼ teaspoon ground red pepper (cayenne), or to taste

1. Whisk together the soy sauce, saké, mirin and sugar in a small bowl until the sugar is dissolved. Set aside.

2. Bring a large stockpot of lightly salted water to a boil. Add the shaved burdock and blanch for 3 minutes. Drain and pat dry.

3. Heat the oil in a large skillet over high heat. Add the blanched burdock and carrots and sauté, stirring continuously, for 3 minutes. Add the soy sauce mixture and continue to stir until most of the liquid is absorbed, about 2 minutes. Remove the pan from the heat and mix in the toasted sesame seeds and *shichimi togarashi*. Serve warm or at room temperature.

Cooking Tips *As you're preparing the burdock, place the cleaned pieces in a bowl of acidulated water (water with a small amount of lemon juice or vinegar added) to keep it from discoloring. To ensure that the oil is hot enough to start sautéing, dip a carrot piece into the oil—it's ready when tiny bubbles sizzle around its edges.*

Fried Potatoes with Miso and Sesame

These crispy fried potatoes are tossed with a thick miso paste. At first taste, the miso flavor may seem too subtle. But this is intentional as the flavor strengthens with each additional bite.

SERVES 4 AS A SIDE DISH

- 1 lb (500 g) unpeeled baby red ("new") potatoes, sliced into ¼-in (6-mm)-thick rounds, or any variety of larger potatoes, cut lengthwise into halves or quarters (depending on size) and sliced into ¼-in (6-mm)-thick pieces
- 2 tablespoons miso, preferably red
- 2 teaspoons saké
- 1 teaspoon mirin
- ¼ cup (65 ml) oil
- 2 teaspoons toasted sesame seeds (see "Toasting Sesame Seeds," page 16)

1. Blanch the sliced potatoes in salted water for 5 minutes. Drain.

2. Meanwhile, combine the miso, saké and mirin in a small bowl to form a paste. Set aside.

3. Add the oil to a large skillet (12 in/30 cm is best) or wide pot over medium heat. When hot, add the potatoes, stir to coat with oil, and then spread evenly across the pan to create a single layer. Let cook, undisturbed, for 7 minutes. Gently flip with tongs, and cook an additional 5 to 10 minutes, flipping occasionally, until crisp and brown on both sides. Remove the potato rounds as they brown so as not to overcook them.

4. Off heat, add the miso mixture. Gently toss together, being careful not to break apart the potatoes. Sprinkle with the sesame seeds and serve.

Cooking Tip *If you're using the extra-thick hacho miso (as opposed to the suggested red), thin down the paste with an additional 2 teaspoons saké and 1 teaspoon mirin.*

Fried Potatoes with Miso and Sesame

Miso-Slathered Daikon
Daikon Dengaku

Not only is Hiromi an incredibly good cook, she's also an incredibly creative one. This recipe is just one more example that proves it.

Dengaku is a common Japanese dish (and one of my favorites!) that typically consists of grilled, skewered eggplant—although other ingredients, like tofu, can also be used—slathered with miso. The key component to dengaku is the miso sauce.

In Hiromi's version, she takes the traditional preparation one step further, boiling large rounds of fresh daikon in starchy rice water until tender and sweet. She then tops them with the strong, dark *hacho miso*.

SERVES 4

4 cups (1 liter) reserved rice rinsing water (see Cooking Tip at right) or water

1 lb (500 g) daikon, peeled and sliced into 1-in (2.5-cm) rounds

Toasted sesame seeds, for garnish (see "Toasting Sesame Seeds," page 16)

Shiso, thinly sliced, for garnish (optional)

½ recipe White Rice (page 28)

HACHO MISO SAUCE

4 tablespoons miso, preferably hacho

4 tablespoons sugar

2 tablespoons mirin

1 tablespoon saké

1. To make the Hacho Miso Sauce, whisk together the ingredients in a small bowl. Set aside.

2. Bring the reserved rice rinsing water or water to a boil in a large saucepan. Add sliced daikon rounds, reduce the heat to medium, and simmer for 30 minutes, or until fork-tender. Drain and rinse.

3. Spread a thick layer of the Hacho Miso Sauce over each daikon round. If using the thinner daikon available at larger grocery and natural foods stores, you'll want to offer each guest a couple of slices. If using the much heftier and thicker variety found at Asian markets, one sliced round per serving should suffice. Garnish with the sesame seeds and *shiso*, if using. Serve with rice.

Cooking Tip *Be sure to save the milky-colored water leftover from rinsing the rice. Cooking the daikon in this starchy water helps remove any odor and tempers the slight bitter flavor of daikon.*

Deep-Fried Tofu in Sweet Fish Stock
Agedashi Dofu

Although this is a classic Japanese recipe, toppings will vary from household to household. The following is how my friend Atsuko does it.

Mentsuyu—or the more professional term *warishita*—the sauce poured around this fried tofu, is a multi-purpose condiment commonly found in the Japanese kitchen. It's often used on top of *donburi* and other "one-pot" dishes, or as a dipping sauce for boiled *udon* or *somen* noodles.

SERVES 2 TO 4

One 1-lb (500-g) block firm tofu, pressed (see "Pressing Tofu," page 17)
Potato starch or cornstarch
Oil, for deep-frying

MENTSUYU SAUCE
¾ cup (185 ml) Fish Stock (page 26)
4 tablespoons soy sauce
3 tablespoons saké
2 tablespoons mirin
¾ teaspoon sugar

TOPPINGS
Peeled and grated daikon (optional)
Peeled and grated ginger (optional)
Sliced green onions (scallions) (optional)
Dried bonito fish flakes (katsuobushi) (optional)

1. Cut the pressed tofu into four pieces. Blot each with paper towel and coat with potato starch or cornstarch. Set aside on wire rack.

2. Heat 2 to 3 inches (5 to 7.5 cm) oil to 350°F (175°C) in a deep-fryer, stockpot or large wok.

3. To make the Mentsuyu Sauce, bring all the ingredients to a gentle simmer in a small saucepan (do not bring to a full boil).

Cook 1 minute more, and then turn off the heat. Cover and keep warm until ready to use. (When warm, the Mentsuyu Sauce will be better absorbed by the tofu.)

4. Deep-fry the tofu, in batches, until light golden brown, 6 to 8 minutes. Gently flip the tofu halfway through frying. Using a slotted spoon, carefully remove and let drain on a clean wire rack. Repeat with remaining tofu pieces.

5. To serve family style, place the fried tofu pieces in a bowl, top with preferred garnishes, and then pour the warm Mentsuyu Sauce around the edge of the tofu, so as not to disturb the toppings. If you wish to serve individual portions, place one or two fried tofu pieces in a bowl, garnish and pour about ¼ cup (65 ml) of the warm sauce around the tofu pieces.

Cooking Tips *Since tofu is considered a prepared food, you're essentially just crisping the outside and not as concerned about cooking the interior. Use fresh, clean oil when deep-frying to prevent dark spots from appearing on the tofu, as this is both unattractive and unappetizing.*

See "Deep-Frying 101" on page 17 for more tips.

Japanese-Style Vegetable Gratin

Whether served savory or sweet, gratins are fusion dishes that are gaining popularity all over Japan. But it was the box of local, organic produce that Hiromi's farmer friend gave her that inspired this tofu-vegetable version.

SERVES 4 TO 6

½ kabocha (Japanese pumpkin) (about 8 oz/250 g), unpeeled and sliced into ½ or ¼ moons, depending on size (about 2 cups)

½ block (8 oz/250 g) soft tofu

2 cups (120 g) thinly sliced fresh mushrooms (like eringi or shiitake)

1 small sweet potato, peeled, sliced in half moons (about 1 cup)

1 large carrot, peeled, sliced in half moons (about 1 cup)

2 cups (190 g) broccoli florets

1 cup (250 ml) soy milk

3 tablespoons miso

1 chicken bouillon cube

1 teaspoon freshly ground white pepper, or to taste

½ teaspoon salt, or to taste

½ cup (40 g) thinly sliced leek

2 oz (60 g) shredded mozzarella cheese (about ½ cup)

2 slices uncooked bacon, thinly sliced

2 tablespoons butter, cut into small cubes, plus additional butter for greasing dish

2 tablespoons panko (Japanese bread crumbs)

1. Preheat the oven to 400°F (200°C).

2. Dry roast the *kabocha* in a large skillet over medium heat until lightly browned, about 5 minutes.

3. Blanch the tofu in a large pot of lightly salted boiling water for 3 minutes. Remove with a slotted spoon. Let cool to the touch and then squeeze gently to eliminate excess moisture. Set aside.

4. Using the same pot of water, blanch in batches the mushrooms, sweet potato, carrot and broccoli florets until their color "pops" (intensifies) and they just start to turn tender. For best results, use these

suggested times: mushrooms (30 seconds), broccoli florets (1 minute), carrots (2 minutes), sweet potato (3 minutes). Set aside.

5. Puree the blanched tofu, soy milk and miso in a blender until smooth. Pour the mixture into a large saucepan. Over medium-low heat, add the bouillon and, stirring occasionally to prevent burning, heat through until dissolved, about 5 minutes. Add the salt and pepper.

6. Add the blanched sweet potatoes, carrots, and mushrooms and stir gently until completely coated in the sauce. Remove from the heat.

7. Using a slotted spoon, transfer the sauce-coated vegetables into a lightly buttered 9-inch (23-cm) ceramic pie pan or baking dish. Reserve the sauce.

8. Lightly coat the kabocha and broccoli in the remaining sauce, then arrange on top of the other vegetables.

9. Sprinkle the leek, cheese and bacon over the top. Dot with the cubed butter, and top with the *panko*.

10. Bake for 20 minutes, or until the edges are bubbly and the top is golden brown. Serve immediately.

Cooking Tips *If you can't find kabocha (Japanese pumpkin), use peeled acorn or butternut squash, instead.*

This dish does not reheat well, so plan to enjoy it at its best—straight from the oven.

The tofu in this recipe is blanched before using. As shared in The Book of Tofu & Miso by William Shurtleff and Akiko Aoyagi, there are a number of reasons for blanching tofu. Blanching tofu warms the tofu through; it freshens stored tofu that shows signs of spoilage; and, it makes the tofu slightly firmer so that when simmered in seasoned broths it

absorbs flavors without diluting the cooking liquid. Using lightly salted water, as called for in this recipe, helps firm up the tofu's texture as well.

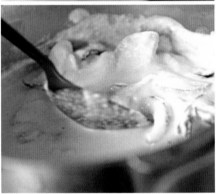

"Katsuo no Tataki" Fried Eggplant Salad

Everyone I asked about *Katsuo no Tataki* just got this look in their eyes, this look of knowing, and that soon I would know too—like it's some sort of club; this look of envy because they weren't able to join me in the culinary adventure . . . so there was simply no way I was not going to go check out this dish firsthand. And that's when I realized that it's not until you actually try Katsuo no Tataki at the source—in Kochi city on Shikoku, among the crowds of a frenetic Sunday market—that you appreciate how utterly amazing perfection really is.

The Kochi open-air Sunday market makes the trip even more worthwhile. First opened in 1690, it's said to be the oldest market in Japan—that still opens regularly—and it runs along the picturesque tree-lined boulevard leading up to the city's castle. Informal by nature, the lively market is colored by the crowd's different intentions: people shoving, dawdling, hurrying, negotiating, visiting; having to dance your way around shopping carts, oversized backpacks, and bicycles; all in a narrow area full of seasonal fruits and vegetables, locally produced ice cream, and eager merchants' calls. This is a market like it's supposed to be.

But just off the strip, in an industrial warehouse close to the castle, lies the real gem, the Hirome Market. While the Sunday market sells the goods to make the food, the Hirome Market sells the food waiting to be eaten! Its unassuming food court is filled with noisy children, rebellious teenagers, lunching ladies, and working men

boisterously drinking away their Sunday holiday. That they are all fighting for space at the overflowing picnic tables confirms that you were the last to be let in on the secret. The secret is that it's here that one of the best meals in Japan is served: Katsuo no Tataki.

Katsuo (skipjack tuna) is, hands down, my favorite fish in Japan. And it is in Kochi city that they've mastered the art of preparing it. Katsuo no Tataki is essentially nothing more than katsuo, so briefly char-grilled it's basically served raw like sashimi, while long enough to become infused with an impressively bold, smoky flavor. It is, without a doubt, worth a trip to Kochi just to eat it. Unfortunately, preparing Katsuo no Tataki for a weeknight meal at home is not terribly practical. I was therefore elated when my friend Atsuko, who equally appreciates the dish, taught me this deliciously adequate (and by far much easier) variation. Atsuko's recipe comes from her sister-in-law who lives in Shikoku. She simply substituted the similarly colored deep-fried eggplant for the katsuo.

For this dish, Atusko uses a mirin-sweetened *sanbaizu*—an easy, all-purpose sauce made of three (*san* means "three") ingredients: equal parts of soy sauce, rice wine vinegar and sugar or mirin. Atsuko chose to use mirin in this recipe so that there would be more liquid with which to marinate the eggplant.

SERVES 4

3 Japanese eggplants
Oil, for deep-frying
½ onion, thinly sliced
3 to 4 shiso leaves, thinly sliced, for garnish (optional)
1 recipe White Rice (page 28)

SANBAIZU SAUCE
3 tablespoons mirin
3 tablespoons soy sauce
3 tablespoons rice wine vinegar
2 cloves garlic, grated

1. To make the Sanbaizu Sauce, whisk together the mirin, soy sauce, vinegar and grated garlic in a small bowl. Set aside.

2. Slice the eggplants in half lengthwise. Using the tip of a sharp knife, score the purple skin diagonally along the length of the eggplants. Repeat in the opposite direction as if making an "X." There will now be a number of small squares in the eggplants' purple skin. The eggplant can be deep-fried as is or, for a more informal presentation, slice into 1-inch (2.5-cm) bite-size chunks.

3. Heat 2 inches (5 cm) of oil to 375°F (190°C) in a deep-fryer, stockpot or large wok. Add the eggplant—in batches so as not to crowd—and deep-fry, stirring gently, until browned, 1 to 2 minutes (eggplant halves may take a little longer). (Watch the oil temperature carefully—you may need to let the oil come back to temperature between frying each batch of eggplant.) Remove the eggplant with a slotted spoon and set in a single layer on a paper towel–lined tray. Repeat with the remaining eggplant.

4. To arrange, place the fried eggplant chunks or halves skin-side up in a shallow serving dish. Pour the Sanbaizu Sauce over; top with the sliced onions and garnish with the thinly sliced *shiso*. Serve with rice.

Cooking Tips *Since the onion is served raw, it's best to use a mild, sweet onion, such as a Vidalia. If none are available, or if the taste of any raw onion is considered too harsh, toss the sliced onions with salt, let sit a few minutes, and then rinse in cool water and gently squeeze dry. This helps mellow their flavor.*

Be sure to leave the suggested amount of headroom in your pan when deep-frying the eggplant. The natural moisture in the eggplant will cause the oil to bubble up when frying.

See "Deep-Frying 101" on page 17 for more tips.

Savory Tofu Patties

Ganmodoki

The first time I had *Ganmodoki*, my dear friend Hitomi showed up at my door around dinnertime with a wooden tray filled with five or six different courses all artistically arranged in perfectly matching pottery. (I was twenty-eight years old, and this family *still* made it a priority to be sure I was fed each night!) While everything she brought was delicious, the Savory Tofu Patties her mom had made for me—deep-fried until light golden brown, filled with soft tofu and crunchy vegetables—stood out from the very first bite.

Hitomi's mom originally made this recipe with one sheet of *hanpen*, a light, puffy cake made of ground fish. Hanpen is especially popular in Nagasaki, where it is a common ingredient in the local dish *Chanpon*. But since it is not widely available outside of large Asian markets in the West, and the recipe tastes delicious without it, I omitted it from the ingredient list.

These rice patties are even tastier when served with the Sanbaizu Sauce that is part of the "Katsuo no Tataki" Fried Eggplant Salad (page 134). For a refreshing contrast to the fried patties, serve with *shishito*, a tiny green pepper that looks like a hot chili but is deceptively sweet. If unavailable, sliced green bell pepper is an adequate substitute.

Savory Tofu Patties

MAKES 8 PATTIES

10 oz (300 g) firm tofu, pressed (see "Pressing Tofu," page 17)

Scant ¼ cup (5 g) dried, shredded tree ear mushrooms

½ cup (60 g) peeled and diced lotus root, dabbed dry with a paper towel

¼ cup (40 g) peeled and diced carrot, dabbed dry with a paper towel

1 tablespoon potato starch or cornstarch

1 tablespoon soy sauce

1 teaspoon salt

1 egg

Oil, for deep-frying

1 recipe Sanbaizu Sauce (replace garlic with 1 heaping tablespoon peeled and grated daikon) (page 134)

Shishito or sliced green pepper (optional)

1. While the tofu is being pressed, prepare the mushrooms. Place the tree ear mushrooms in a small heat-proof bowl. Pour boiling water over them, cover with plastic wrap so that the plastic is touching the surface of the water, and let steep for 30 minutes, or until softened. (If you are unable to find dried, shredded tree ear mushrooms, simply buy whole, and then slice thinly once softened.) Drain and dab dry with paper towels.

2. Mash the pressed tofu with the back of a fork in a medium bowl. Or, use a mortar and pestle. Add the mushrooms, lotus root, carrot, starch, soy sauce, salt, and egg and stir to combine.

3. Using a ¼-cup (65-ml) measure, form 8 balls.

4. Heat 2 inches (5 cm) of oil to 350°F (175°C) in a deep-fryer, stockpot or large wok. Gently add the balls to the hot oil and deep-fry, in batches, until golden brown, about 3 minutes. Using a slotted spoon, carefully remove and let drain on a clean wire rack. Repeat with remaining balls.

5. Serve warm or at room temperature with the Sanbaizu Sauce and shishito, if using.

Cooking Tips *As the tofu needs to be pressed and the mushrooms rehydrated before using, be sure to plan accordingly. Once these ingredients are prepped, it doesn't take long to make the tofu balls.*

The lotus root will discolor quickly after being diced. If not using immediately, keep in acidulated water (water mixed with a small amount of lemon juice or white vinegar) until ready to use. For a silkier consistency, grind the tofu, starch, soy sauce, salt and egg in a suribachi (ribbed mortar, see page 12) or food processor until smooth. Transfer to a bowl and stir in the vegetables.

See "Deep-Frying 101" on page 17 for more tips.

Seasoned Taro Root
Yaki Satoimo no Kurabu

While staying in Obuse, I treated myself to dinner at the local (and famous) saké distillery. And to this day, it remains one of the best experiences I've had yet in Japan: the dark, cavernous room quietly crowded with parties equally enjoying both their dinner and their companions; the large wooden counter encircling the open kitchen where the archaic cooking methods the restaurant is famous for preserving are put on display (and where, of course, I sat to get an up-close-and-personal view); plus too many glasses of the house-made beer, which led to innocent flirtations with the waiter and the courage to ask for this recipe!

SERVES 4

12 taro root (each about 2 in/5 cm long) or small potatoes, peeled
1½ cups (375 ml) Fish Stock (page 26)
½ cup (125 ml) soy sauce
6 tablespoons saké
4 tablespoons mirin
1½ teaspoons peeled and grated ginger
2 tablespoons peeled and grated daikon
1½ teaspoons sugar
Oil, for deep-frying

1. Bring a large pot of water to a boil. Add the peeled taro root and boil 15 minutes, or until fork-tender but not mushy. Drain. Roll the taro root in paper towel to dry. (When cooked, taro root can take on a harmless purple-ish hue. If this happens after boiling, leave as is or peel away the tinted areas with a vegetable peeler.)

2. Meanwhile, warm the Fish Stock, soy sauce, saké, mirin, ginger, daikon and sugar in a medium saucepan over medium heat. Do not let boil or the Fish Stock will turn bitter. Set aside, cover, and keep warm.

3. Meanwhile, heat 2 inches (5 cm) of oil to 350°F (175°C) in a deep-fryer, stockpot or large wok.

4. Add the taro root, in batches as not to crowd, and deep-fry until light golden, 3 to 5 minutes. Using a slotted spoon, carefully remove and let drain on a clean wire rack. Repeat with remaining taro root.

5. Increase the heat to 375°F (190°C). To create an extra-crispy skin, fry the taro root a second time at a higher temperature. Add the taro root, in batches, and fry until golden, 1 to 2 minutes more. Using a slotted spoon, carefully remove and let drain on a clean wire rack. Repeat with remaining taro root.

6. To serve, place three fried taro root pieces in the center of a bowl. Pour the warm, seasoned Fish Stock around the fried taro root (it should come about one-third the way up the taro root, or about ½-inch/1.25-cm deep in the bowl).

Cooking Tips *For best results, purchase the smaller variety of taro root (approximately 2 inches/5 cm in length) or cut the larger variety down to this size. If you can't find taro root, small potatoes can be used.*

Although I've never had any problems, raw taro root is known to irritate some people's skin. As a precautionary measure, you can wear rubber gloves when peeling.

See "Deep-Frying 101" on page 17 for more tips.

Soy Sauce Marinated Fava Beans
Shoyumame

Most great inventions come about by accident, and as the legend goes, the creation of *Shoyumame* was no different: One day, a woman was patiently roasting fava beans when one popped out of the pan and into a bowl of soy sauce. As fate would have it, unnoticed or forgotten, the bean remained in the sauce. Later, when she discovered the bean, she tasted it and was surprised by how delicious it was. And the rest, as they say, is Shoyumame history. Before coming to visit Takamatsu, I mentioned to the Goodwill Guides—Shizuka and Hiroko—that I was really interested in trying the beans the area is famous for. With a moderate temperature and rich soil, Kagawa Prefecture (of which Takamatsu is the capital city) has a good environment for growing fava beans. And as we were finishing our big, slurpy bowls of *Sanuki Udon* (another of the area's famed dishes, see "Sanuki Udon," page 87), the guides surprised me with a small plastic container full of these beans. Since Shoyumame is mainly found in home kitchens, Hiroko had her ninety-one-year-old mother-in-law make up a batch just for me to try!

Eaten with chopsticks or skewered with toothpicks, the marinated beans are typically served as an accompaniment to lunch or dinner. They're also an ideal bar snack when paired with saké or beer. This dish is sweetened more or less to the cook's preference, and sometimes a little spice is added. I usually prepare the beans on the sweet side, with a chili pepper or two added for bite.

MAKES 6 CUPS (1.5 KG)

3 cups (480 g) dried fava beans

SOAKING SOUP
2 cups (500 ml) water
1½ to 2 cups (300 to 400 g) sugar
½ cup (125 ml) soy sauce
2 tablespoons mirin
1 tablespoon saké
1 teaspoon salt
1 chili pepper, deseeded and sliced
(optional)

1. In a large heavy-bottomed skillet over low heat, dry roast the fava beans, stirring occasionally, until dark brown with a strong toasted odor, but not burnt, about 20 minutes.

2. Meanwhile, fill a large enameled Dutch oven or a heavy-bottomed stockpot with water and bring to a boil. Gradually add the hot, roasted beans to the pot. Be careful as the water will bubble vigorously when the hot beans are added. Immediately cover tightly, turn off the heat and let steep for 1 hour. Drain.

3. To make the Soaking Soup, bring all the ingredients to a boil in the same stockpot or Dutch oven used to soak the beans. Add the beans, reduce the heat to medium-low, and simmer for 20 minutes. Cover tightly; turn off the heat and let steep 2 hours to overnight. (No need to drain the beans after steeping. Most of the liquid will have been absorbed, and that which remains is a tasty coating.)

4. Enjoy the beans whole, or pop them out of their skin before eating. Refrigerate any extras in an airtight container.

Cooking Tips *These beans are best when made with the large varietal of dried fava beans—I found mine at a local Italian grocery store. For this recipe, it is also best to use enameled cast-iron cookware as the material provides an even heat when dry roasting and retains the Soaking Soup heat better while the beans are steeping. For extra spice, add a seeded, sliced chili pepper (or two!) to the Soaking Soup. The sweetness of the beans depends on how much sugar you use. If a sweeter flavor is preferred, add the full 2 cups.*

Special Equipment *Dutch oven or heavy-bottomed stockpot with tight-fitting lid*

Purple from Head to Toe

"What's your color?" Shizuka, one of the Goodwill Guides I was to meet up with in Takamatsu, asked me over the phone? Not really sure what she meant, I told her blue, the first color that sprung to mind. "Well," she said, "mine's purple. So just look for that when we try finding each other at the train station Tuesday."

Little did I realize how purple Shizuka really was! Anxiously awaiting my arrival, I stepped off the train at 12:08 PM and there was Shizuka's smiling face with her purple shoes, purple dress and purple-streaked hair! Purple bags, purple name cardholder and purple pen . . . she really meant it when she said purple was her color, and I was immediately put at ease by the fun-loving figure standing before me.

Spicy Pan-Seared Eggplant

I was introduced to this recipe while staying with my friend Michiko in Fukuoka, an inlet town on the southern island of Kyushu known for its *karashimentaiko* (spicy salted cod roe). Although Shizuka, Michiko's eighty-five-year-old mother, kept apologizing for her daughter's menu choice—acknowledging my interest in local specialties and this recipe's lack of traditional roots—I thought it was a deliciously creative combination and devoured half the platter myself.

SERVES 4 AS A SIDE DISH

2 Japanese eggplants (each about 12 in/30 cm long)

1 tablespoon oil

¼ cup (28 g) shredded mozzarella cheese

4 teaspoons prepared spicy salted cod roe (karashimentaiko), see page 50 for instructions (optional)

¼ cup (65 ml) soy sauce, preferably dark

1. Peel the eggplants lengthwise, alternating rows to form purple and white stripes. (See top photograph on right.) Slice the eggplants into rounds, about ¼ to ½-in (6-mm to 1.25-cm) thick.

2. Heat the oil in a 12-inch (30-cm) nonstick skillet over medium-high heat. When hot, add the eggplant slices and cook until browned on one side, 3 to 5 minutes. Flip, and cook 1 minute more. Top each slice with about 1 teaspoon cheese and ¼ teaspoon roe, if using. Cover the pan and let cook until the cheese melts, about 1 minute.

3. Remove from the heat and immediately pour the soy sauce into the hot pan. The heat from the pan will caramelize the soy sauce and release its flavors. Once the sauce has reduced and the bubbling subsided (about 1 minute), remove the eggplant from the pan, place on a platter, drizzle over any of the remaining sauce, and serve.

Cooking Tips *If doubling the recipe, you'll need to have multiple pans, or allot for cleaning time since the pan must be cleaned before reusing.*

If you're not using a nonstick pan, increase the oil to 2 tablespoons.

Although okay to use "regular" soy sauce, dark soy sauce is preferred. Thicker in consistency, it adds a more pronounced color to the dish along with a noticeable molasses flavor. Dark soy sauce is sweeter and less salty than the traditional variety.

Special Equipment *Nonstick skillet (12 in/30 cm) with cover*

CHAPTER 7

Desserts and Drinks

I'm one of those people who has to have chocolate every day. So, of course, I was a little nervous about moving to Japan, having no idea how I was going to get my daily fix.

What little I knew!

Soon after arriving in the country, it became obvious that Japan is home to a wide array of delectable sweet treats. From the traditional *yokan* and *mochi*, to the fusion soft creams—served in such bizarre but utterly delicious flavors as soy sauce, miso and chestnut—even the candy aisle in the grocery store was home to local twists like green-tea Kit Kats. And don't get me started on Meiji-brand's way-too-addictive chocolate-covered almonds . . . .

The Japanese even have a phrase, *betsu bara*, used to describe the "separate stomach" available just for desert. I had nothing to worry about!

What follows is a collection of uniquely Japanese desserts along with some delicious drink recipes that I discovered during my travels. While Japanese green tea quickly became a daily ritual, I was surprised to find these great-tasting alternatives, as well. *Itadakimasu*! (Bon appétit!)

OoLong Tea Chiffon Cake

This is Hitomi's cake. For any celebration that arises, she's called on to make it. Her aunt, Hiromi, has employed her to keep the restaurant well stocked with its various flavors (try the Banana Chiffon Cake, see opposite page), and one day, Hitomi hopes to make her own business out of it.

Like most Japanese desserts, it's still fairly good for you—or not that bad for you, depending on how you look at your glass. But the thing I like most about this chiffon cake is that it's simple. When making the cake, you can use whatever type of tea you prefer. I like the flavor of Oolong, while Hitomi favors Earl Grey. Or, if she has any on-hand, her favorite is to use a black tea–blue cornflower tea blend.

This cake tastes very nice on its own. It's great for snacking or slicing a piece for your lunchbox. But for an extra-special touch—like when celebrating her father-in-law's birthday—Hitomi will frost the cake, as well (as shown in this recipe).

SERVES 12

3 tablespoons loose leaf oolong tea, or 4 tea bags, divided
²/₃ cup (160 ml) water
4 egg yolks
³/₄ cup (150 g) sugar, divided
¼ cup (65 ml) vegetable oil
½ teaspoon salt
1 cup plus 2 tablespoons (140 g) cake flour (not self-rising), sifted
6 egg whites, room temperature
Pinch of salt

FROSTING (OPTIONAL)
1 cup (250 ml) heavy cream
2 tablespoons powdered sugar

1. Preheat the oven to 325°F (160°C) with the rack in the middle position.

2. Using a mortar and pestle or an electric coffee grinder, grind 1 tablespoon of the loose leaf tea until fine. Set aside. If you're using tea bags, skip this step.

3. Bring the water to a boil in a small saucepan. Add the remaining 2 tablespoons of loose leaf tea or, if using, the 4 tea bags. Cover and let steep according to packaged instructions, about 5 minutes. Strain if using loose leaf tea. Let cool to room temperature. If necessary, add additional water to measure ²/₃ cup (160 ml).

4. Whisk together the egg yolks, ½ cup (100 g) of the sugar, oil, salt, ground tea leaves and steeped tea in a large bowl. Add the flour and gently whisk just until smooth. Set aside.

5. Beat the egg whites in another large bowl with an electric mixer on medium speed. When the whites become frothy, add the salt. When the whites begin to increase in volume and lose their opaqueness, gradually add the remaining ¼ cup (50 g) sugar. Beat until whites are stiff and glossy, but not dry.

6. Fold ¼ of the whites into the egg yolk-tea mixture to loosen the batter, then gently fold in the remaining whites just until fully incorporated, being careful not to deflate.

7. Pour batter into an ungreased 10-inch (25-cm) tube pan with removable bottom.

Gently run a knife or spatula through the batter to break up any large air pockets—be sure to reach the bottom.

8. Bake for 30 to 35 minutes, or until a toothpick inserted in the middle comes out clean. Let cool upside down—suspended over the neck of a wine bottle works best.

9. Once the cake is completely cooled, remove it from the pan by running a knife around the sides and carefully pushing the bottom out. To release the tube portion from the cake, carefully run a knife between the cake and bottom of the pan.

10. To make the optional Frosting, beat together the cream and sugar in a bowl with an electric mixer on medium-high speed until soft peaks form.

11. The outside of the cake can be quite crumbly. To keep the frosting crumb-free, spread a thin layer of the whipped cream over the cooled cake. Refrigerate the cake (and remaining whipped cream) until set—5 to 10 minutes. Then frost the cake with the remaining whipped cream. The cake should be frosted just before serving.

Baking Tips *For an extra light and airy chiffon cake, Hitomi sifts the flour 6 to 7 times after measuring—a technique I have since adopted myself.*

The cake is best prepared with loose leaf tea. But if using tea bags, steep the tea while it's still in the bags—if you cut them open, the ground leaves will soak up too much of the water.

As noted in The Baker's Dozen Cookbook, *edited by Rick Rodgers, when preparing a chiffon cake, do not grease the pan. For maximum volume, the batter needs traction to climb up the sides of the pan. For this same reason, do not use a pan with a nonstick surface.*

So as not to smoosh the delicate texture of the cake, slice with a serrated or electric knife.

Special Equipment *10-inch (25-cm) tube pan with removable bottom*

Banana Chiffon Cake

All-purpose flour is called for in this recipe (as opposed to the cake flour in Oolong Tea Chiffon Cake, page 142) to support the weight of the banana. For a light and airy cake, sift the flour six to seven times after measuring.

SERVES 12

1 very ripe banana
2 to 4 tablespoons milk
4 egg yolks
³/₄ cup (150 g) sugar
¼ cup (65 ml) vegetable oil
½ teaspoon salt
½ teaspoon vanilla
1 cup (145 g) all-purpose flour, sifted
1 cup (250 ml) egg whites, room temperature (from 7 to 8 large eggs)
Pinch of salt

1. Preheat the oven to 325°F (160°C) with the rack in the middle position.

2. In a clear measuring cup, mash together the banana and enough milk to total ²/₃ cup (160 ml).

3. Whisk together the banana mixture, egg yolks, ½ cup (100 g) of the sugar, oil, salt and vanilla in a large bowl. Add the flour and gently whisk just until smooth. Set aside.

4. Beat the egg whites in another large bowl with an electric mixer on medium speed. When the whites become frothy, add the salt. When the whites begin to increase in volume and lose their opaqueness, gradually add the remaining ¼ cup (50 g) sugar. Beat until the whites are stiff and glossy, but not dry.

5. Fold ¼ of the whites into the banana mixture to loosen the batter, then gently fold in the remaining whites just until fully incorporated, being careful not to deflate.

6. Pour the batter into an ungreased 10-inch (25-cm) tube pan with removable bottom. Gently run a knife or spatula through the batter to break up any large air pockets—be sure to reach the bottom.

7. Follow steps 8 through 11 for Oolong Tea Chiffon Cake (page 142) for baking, cooling and icing the cake, if using frosting.

Green Tea Snow Cone

Hiromi ended her Japanese-themed cooking class with this traditional summertime sweet. Since the focal point of this recipe is the *matcha* (unsweetened green tea powder), use the highest quality you can find. The snow cone will only taste as good as the matcha used.

SERVES 4

1 cup (250 ml) water
1 cup (200 g) sugar
2 tablespoons matcha (unsweetened green tea powder) (see page 155)
4 cups (500 g) shaved ice (see Cooking Tips, below)

1. In a small saucepan, bring the water and sugar to a boil. Reduce the heat and simmer for 3 minutes. Swirl the pan occasionally to help dissolve the sugar. Remove the pan from the heat.

2. In a small bowl, whisk together ¼ cup (65 ml) of the hot sugar syrup with the matcha until dissolved. Return this green tea concentrate back to the saucepan and stir to combine.

3. Strain the mixture through a fine-mesh sieve into a small bowl, cover with plastic wrap and refrigerate until chilled.

4. Mound the shaved ice into four serving bowls. Drizzle with the chilled green tea syrup and serve.

5. Store any leftover syrup in an air-tight container in the refrigerator for up to 1 month.

Cooking Tips *To preserve green tea's vibrant green color, avoid excess exposure to heat. For this reason, use Elizabeth Andoh's method of adding a small amount of the hot syrup to "temper" the tea before adding it to the rest of the mixture.*

If you don't have access to a snow-cone maker or shaved ice machine, you can use a food processor (a blender won't work). Process a few cubes at a time (it will be loud!), storing the shaved ice in the freezer until the full 4 cups have been made.

Special Equipment *Fine-mesh sieve, or cheesecloth or coffee filter to line colander; snow-cone maker, shaved ice machine or food processor*

Polar Bear Snow Cone
Shirokuma

Any reference to *Shirokuma* seems to guarantee an automatic response—comic pantomime included—mimicking the painful effects of brain freeze. This creative version of the Japanese snow cone is from Kagoshima, at the southern tip of Kyushu. The name, literally "white (*shiro*) bear (*kuma*)," is derived from the dessert's snowy color. The fruit is added to liven it up. When I told Michiko I was on the hunt for Shirokuma, we ended up finding only the pre-packaged variety in the frozen foods section at her local grocery store. Disappointingly, it looked like nothing more than a skimpy scoop of ice cream, garnished with one lonely slice of canned orange. When I finally made my way further south to the original store where this legendary snow cone was created, I was much more impressed—and a little intimidated—by the overwhelming presentation. The "small" that I ordered came in a cup overflowing with a mound of glazed ice three times its size. Amazingly, this was then gravity-defyingly decorated with one triangular slice each of honeydew and watermelon, a few raisins, a couple pink and green squares of gelatin, one prune, one round banana slice, some mandarin oranges, a slice of pineapple and one white bean to finish it off. Phew! I don't expect you to serve this snow cone the traditional way. Though a large assortment of fruits and other colorful garnishes does make for an impressive presentation, it also requires time-consuming preparation. Instead, decorate the snow cone with whatever fruits, berries, or other sweets you have on hand.

SERVES 4

½ cup (125 ml) water
¼ cup (50 g) sugar
1 cup (250 ml) sweetened condensed milk
4 cups (500 g) shaved ice (see Cooking Tips, left)
Assorted fruit, for garnish

1. In a small saucepan, bring the water and sugar to a boil. Reduce the heat and simmer for 3 minutes. Swirl the pan occasionally to help dissolve the sugar. Pour the syrup into a small heatproof bowl or measuring cup. Cover with plastic wrap and refrigerate until chilled.

2. Whisk together the sugar syrup and sweetened condensed milk in a small bowl.

3. Mound the shaved ice into 4 serving bowls. Drizzle with the milk mixture, decorate with fruit, and serve.

Special Equipment *Snow-cone maker, shaved ice machine or food processor*

Sugared Bread Sticks
Pan no Mimi Oyatsu

SERVES 4 TO 6

6 slices white sandwich bread
Sugar to coat the fried bread strips (about 1 cup/200 g)
Oil, for deep-frying

I read somewhere that an additional 30,000 homes could be built each year with the number of *waribashi* (disposable wooden chopsticks) that are thrown away. After discussing this statistic with Hiromi, she told me about *Pan no Mimi Oyatsu*, a guilt-ridden attempt at making up for this utensil waste.

After mothers make sandwiches for their children's lunch boxes each morning, they're left with a pile of crusts. (Yes, they really do eat sandwiches in Japan.) Supposedly, Hiromi laughed, it's this particular dessert that evolved as a way to "recycle" the continued excess. A few days later, now conscious of this frugality, I noticed there were bags of bread crusts at the local bakery quite possibly being sold for just this purpose.

Think of this recipe as quick-and-easy, down-and-dirty home-cooked doughnuts—it's nothing more than deep-fried sandwich bread sprinkled with sugar. And trust me, you will be amazed at how good deep-fried sandwich bread can taste.

Body Part Nomenclature: Although the ends of the bread loaf are referred to as the "heel" in the United States, in Japan they are called the *mimi*, or "ear." Hence the name of this dessert: Pan no Mimi Oyatsu. (*Pan* means "bread" and *oyatsu* means "snack.")

1. Preheat the oven to 350°F (175°C) with the rack in the middle position.
2. Remove the crusts from the bread and set aside. Slice the remaining bread into strips, about 3 x ½-inch (8 x 1.25-cm).
3. Bake the bread strips and crusts on an ungreased baking sheet until dry and toasted, but not browned, about 8 minutes. Cool.
4. Meanwhile, heat the oil to 350°F (175°C) in a deep-fryer, stockpot or large wok.
5. Add the toasted bread and fry, in batches so as not to crowd, until deep golden on both sides, 10 to 20 seconds. To ensure that it cooks evenly, you will need to gently stir and flip the bread as it fries. Using a slotted spoon or chopsticks, transfer the crusts from the hot oil onto a paper towel–lined plate and sprinkle both sides of the bread liberally with sugar (about 2 tablespoons). Repeat with remaining bread strips.
6. Place the fried, sugared bread in a large bowl and toss with additional sugar, if desired. Serve warm.

Cooking Tips *In the spirit of this thrifty recipe, if you don't have an abundance of bread crusts on hand, or don't intend to produce an assembly line of crustless sandwiches, it's quite alright to use the entire slice of bread as this recipe reflects.*

See "Deep-Frying 101" on page 17 for more tips.

Crispy Buckwheat Cookies
Soba Bouro

Portugese in origin, *Soba Bouro* gained popularity in Japan during the Edo Period (1603-1867). Made from buckwheat flour, the cookies are popular in all soba-producing regions of Japan and especially in Kyoto, known for, among other things, its confections. These crisp little flower-shaped cookies have just a hint of sweetness that leaves you wanting for more. Be careful, they become surprisingly addictive! Serve with coffee or tea, dunking the cookies between bites.

MAKES ABOUT 15 COOKIES

¼ cup plus 2 tablespoons (50 g) cake flour

¼ cup plus 2 tablespoons (50 g) buck-wheat flour

½ teaspoon baking soda

½ teaspoon salt

¼ cup plus 5 teaspoons (70 g) sugar

1 egg

1. Place rack in bottom third of oven and preheat to 375°F (190°C).

2. Sift together the cake and buckwheat flours, baking soda and salt in a small bowl.

3. Whisk together the sugar and egg in a medium bowl. Add the flour mixture and stir with a spatula to combine. The batter will be thick but still spreadable.

4. Using the spatula, scoop the batter into a pastry bag. (If you don't have a pastry bag, see Baking Tips, right.)

5. On a parchment-lined baking sheet, pipe 5 dime-size rounds of batter into a connecting circle, leaving a small hole in the center. Repeat with the remaining batter, spacing cookies 1 inch (2.5 cm) apart.

6. Bake for 7 to 10 minutes, rotating pan halfway through baking, or until the cookies are slightly puffed and golden around the edges.

7. Immediately slide the parchment paper and cookies to a cooling rack. They will crisp as they cool. Store in an airtight container.

Baking Tips *Buckwheat flour is available at natural food stores and larger grocery stores. If desired, use white (as opposed to "whole") buckwheat flour for a milder flavor and lighter color.*

A plastic sandwich bag makes a good alternative to a pastry bag. But for this recipe, it won't work. The batter is too thick and will rip the bag, creating a frustrating mess. If you don't have a pastry bag, simply make drop cookies: Drop 2 teaspoons of batter per cookie onto the parchment-lined baking sheet. Bake as directed, erring on the longer side of 10 minutes.

Special Equipment *Parchment paper; pastry bag with plain round tip*

Crispy Buckwheat Cookies

Toasted Sesame Cookies
Goma Kukki

These delicate, crisp cookies are a Reiko-original. They are for sale, wrapped in clear plastic bags and tied with bright red bows, in a basket by the register of the local café where she's been cooking for years.

MAKES 10 DOZEN

²/₃ cup (85 g) toasted white sesame seeds
¹/₃ cup (43 g) toasted black sesame seeds
½ teaspoon salt
1 cup (200 g) sugar
1 egg white
½ cup (1 stick/115 g) unsalted butter, melted

1. Preheat the oven to 350°F (175°C) with the racks positioned in the upper and lower thirds.

2. In a medium bowl, add each ingredient, one at a time, stirring to combine after each addition. Let the mixture rest 15 minutes at room temperature to allow the butter to cool and the batter to solidify.

3. Using a ½-teaspoon measure, drop the batter onto two parchment-lined baking sheets, leaving 3 inches (7.5 cm) between each cookie. The batter will spread a lot during baking.

4. Bake two sheets of cookies at a time, for 7 to 10 minutes, or until deep golden brown, rotating the pans and switching their position halfway through baking. Slide the parchment paper and cookies onto a rack to cool and repeat with the remaining batter. Make sure you use a completely cool pan before dropping any new batter.

5. Store in an airtight container.

Baking 101

• *Read through each recipe before beginning.*

• *Before starting to make the recipe, prepare and measure all of the ingredients and have them at the ready within easy reach (this is a French technique called mise en place, and it is especially helpful when baking).*

• *Unless otherwise stated, all ingredients should be at room temperature (e.g., eggs, milk, butter).*

• *About eggs: Egg whites produce the greatest volume when beaten at room temperature. It's easiest to separate eggs when still cold from the refrigerator (there's less chance of breaking the yolk). If you get any egg yolk in the whites when separating the eggs, use the cracked eggshell to remove it—it has a magnetic-like attraction that makes the broken yolk much easier to remove.*

• *When making a whipped cream frosting, for the best results, chill the cream, beaters and bowl ahead of time.*

Baking Tips *The white and black sesame seeds can be toasted together in the same pan (see "Toasting Sesame Seeds," page 16). If you don't want to bake the entire batch of cookies at once—it makes 10 dozen—the excess batter will keep in the freezer for up to one month. Thaw in the refrigerator and bring to room temperature before using.*

Special Equipment *Parchment paper*

Green Tea Ice Cream with Black Sugar Syrup Matcha Aisu

Green tea and black sugar is a classic pairing in Japan—even the local Denny's restaurant offers the combination on its dessert menu. The recipe that follows is a tribute to a Häagen Dazs ice cream novelty available at any one of the numerous convenience stores, and which I treated myself to more than I'd like to admit. Although sold as an ice cream sandwich in its true form—a crisp, flaky wafer sandwiching a creamy layer of black sugar and a thick block of green tea ice cream—this variation is a more kitchen-friendly alternative to the original. As in a tea ceremony, when the grassy green tea is served with *wagashi* (a sweet) to bite into after drinking, here, the bitterness of this green tea ice cream is offset by the deep, molasses-y sweetness of the Black Sugar Syrup, which is poured over the ice cream before serving. To mimic the ice cream sandwich's crisp cookie crust, I like to serve the ice cream and syrup with Toasted Sesame Cookies (page 147), though any crisp cookie will provide a nice contrast of texture.

This sundae combination is the result of a group collaboration: my favorite green tea ice cream recipe, below, is from Elizabeth Andoh's book *Washoku,* the syrup from Hitomi and the Toasted Sesame Cookies from Reiko.

MAKES 1 PINT (290 G) ICE CREAM

1/3 cup (67 g) sugar

1/3 cup (80 ml) water

1/2 teaspoon mirin

2 teaspoons matcha (unsweetened green tea powder) (see page 155)

1/2 cup (125 ml) whole milk

1/2 cup (125 ml) half-and-half

BLACK SUGAR SYRUP

1/2 cup (200 g) Japanese black sugar (kuro zato) or dark brown sugar, packed

1/4 cup (65 ml) water

1. To make the Black Sugar Syrup, stir the black sugar and water together in a small saucepan. Over medium heat, bring the mixture to a boil, whisking until the sugar is completely dissolved. Pour the syrup into a shallow bowl and place in the refrigerator until completely cooled and slightly thickened.

2. To make the ice cream, combine the 1/3 cup (67 g) sugar and 1/3 cup (80 ml) water in a small saucepan. Stir the mixture over low heat to melt the sugar and then continue to simmer for about 5 minutes, or until a bit syrupy. Add the mirin, stir, and remove the pan from the heat.

3. Combine 1 tablespoon of the warm mirin-sugar-water mixture and the matcha in a small bowl and stir until dissolved. Add this sweet tea concentrate to the saucepan and stir until completely blended. To retain optimal aroma and ensure an intense jade color, do not reheat the mixture. Stir in the milk and half-and-half and mix thoroughly.

4. If you are using an ice-cream maker, pour the matcha-and-milk mixture into the machine and follow the manufacturer's instructions for making a soft-set ice cream. For most models, about 10 minutes of chilling and churning should suffice. Pour the semifrozen mixture into a 3-cup (750-ml) freezer-safe container with a snug-fitting lid. Tap the container gently on a countertop to force out any air bubbles that might be trapped below the surface. Cover and freeze for at least 2 hours, or until firm throughout.

5. If you do not have an ice-cream maker, pour the matcha-and-milk mixture into a flat, shallow freezer-safe container, filling it no more than two-thirds full (the mixture will expand). Tap the container gently on a countertop to force out any air bubbles that might be trapped below the surface. Cover and freeze for 1½ hours, or until nearly firm. Transfer the semifrozen mixture to a blender and pulse in a few short spurts. Or, with a handheld electric mixer or a whisk, whip the mixture vigorously in a deep bowl. Return the mixture to the same container, re-cover, and freeze again for another 45 minutes, or until firm (but not rock-hard) throughout. Repeat the blend or whip step one more time to achieve a silkier texture, re-freezing for a short time (about 1 hour) before serving.

6. The final ice cream, whether made with a blender or ice-cream maker, should be smooth but not too hard. When ready to serve, transfer one or two scoops to pre-chilled bowls.

7. Drizzle some of the Black Sugar Syrup over the ice cream before serving. (If the sryup has become too thick while chilling in the refrigerator, whisk to loosen before using.) Serve with a crispy cookie of your choice.

Cooking Tips *If you can find* kuro zato *(Japanese black sugar), use it. It gives the Black Sugar Syrup a much darker hue and stronger molasses flavor than dark brown sugar.*

You may store any extra Black Sugar Syrup in an airtight container in the refrigerator for up to 1 month.

Special Equipment *Ice-cream maker or blender*

Ginger Tea Kuzu-yu

Michiko's mother, Shizuka, learned this recipe from *her* mother-in-law. Although *Kuzu-yu*, named after the starch used to thicken it, is typically served in winter, the drink is just as satisfying in the summer when chilled and served over ice.

Although this drink tends to be sweet—in the local dialect it's often referred to as *ame-yu*, meaning "candy water"—the ratio of sweetness to spicy ginger flavor is based entirely on personal preference, so feel free to adjust the measurements to your liking.

With its strong ginger flavor and unusual consistency, I like to serve this drink in small cups.

MAKES TWO 4-OUNCE (125-ML) SERVINGS

2 teaspoons kudzu, arrowroot, or cornstarch

1 cup (250 ml) plus 1 tablespoon water, divided

1 tablespoon sugar

1 teaspoon ginger juice (see "Making Ginger Juice," page 15)

1. Stir together the kudzu and 1 tablespoon of the water in a small bowl until dissolved. Set aside.

2. Bring the remaining 1 cup (250 ml) of water, sugar, and ginger juice just to a boil in a small saucepan over medium-high heat.

3. Drizzle the dissolved kudzu into the warm sugar water. Stir the boiling mixture constantly for 1 minute—the mixture will turn glossy and transparent and thicken to a consistency similar to egg whites.

4. Remove from the heat. Serve warm in two small cups.

Cooking Tip *Traditionally prepared with kudzu (a thickener from the kudzu, or kuzu, tuber), this drink can also be made with more widely available and less expensive thickeners such as arrowroot or cornstarch.*

Note *If you're lucky enough to have access to yanaka shoga, a fresh ginger available in early summer in Japan, you can use the green stalk as a fun swizzle stick, as shown in the photograph (left).*

Gingerade Shoga-yu

Always the purveyor of fine foods, when Hiromi was just a little girl, she used to set up her *Shoga-yu* stand at the summer street festival near her house. She would chip off ice from big blocks and then pour the sweet ginger syrup over the shavings.

Squeezing an ample supply of ginger juice from freshly grated ginger requires a bit of a time commitment, for which Hiromi's youthful self never had the patience. So her version was definitely on the sweet side.

The sugar cuts down the intensity of the ginger flavor, which allows this refreshing drink to please even the non-ginger lover.

This recipe can easily be increased to serve a crowd. Or why not make extra? The drink will keep in the refrigerator for up to one week.

MAKES TWO 8-OUNCE (250-ML) SERVINGS

1½ cups (375 ml) water
¾ cup (150 g) sugar
2 tablespoons ginger juice (see "Making Ginger Juice," page 15)

1. Combine the water, sugar and ginger juice in a small saucepan. Bring to a boil over medium-high heat, stirring to dissolve the sugar.
2. Strain through a fine-mesh sieve. Serve over ice in two tall glasses.

Cooking Tips *This recipe is easily adjustable to your taste preferences. Use the measurements given above as a guide. If you want it sweeter, add more sugar (or less ginger, as Hiromi does). Spicier? Add more ginger. You can also use temperature to control the intensity of the drink. When served chilled from the refrigerator, the flavor will be more intense but just as delicious. If you prefer a more diluted ginger flavor, pour the just-prepared hot sugar water directly over ice—the melting ice will soften the drink's flavor and thin down its consistency.*

Green Tea Smoothie

With her husband out golfing for the day, Michiko took me on a tour of the town. Just before dinnertime, we ended up at an uncomfortably overcrowded *depachika* (department store food hall) to purchase groceries for the evening's meal. As we jostled our way towards the fresh vegetables, we passed a tucked-in-the-corner kiosk offering refreshing Green Tea Smoothies. Considered impolite to eat or drink while walking around, we quickly found a seat with the throng of exhausted customers refueling with this refreshing drink.

While making this smoothie back home in the US, I have found that adding a small bit of honeydew melon imparts a sweet fruitiness that pairs well with the green tea's bitter, grassy flavor.

SERVES TWO 16-OUNCE (500-ML) SERVINGS

¼ cup (50 g) sugar
¼ cup (65 ml) water
2 teaspoons matcha (unsweetened green tea powder) (see page 155)
1 cup (250 ml) milk
2 cups (300 g) ice cubes (about 14 cubes)
⅓ cup (60 g) diced honeydew melon (optional)

1. Bring the sugar and water just to a boil in a small saucepan. Remove from the heat.
2. Whisk together 1 tablespoon of the sugar syrup with the matcha in a small bowl until dissolved. Return the mixture to the saucepan. Stir in the milk.
3. In a blender, combine the milk-tea mixture with the ice and melon, if using. Pulse until blended and frothy. Serve immediately.

Cooking Tip *To preserve the green tea's vibrant emerald color, avoid excess exposure to heat. For this reason, use Elizabeth Andoh's method of first adding a small amount of the hot sugar syrup to "temper" the tea, before adding it to the rest of the mixture.*

Japanese Apricot Liqueur
Umeshu

year, many households still look forward to the annual tradition of making their own family recipe.

Using a technique learned from *her* mom, Ikuko, Hitomi's mother-in-law, makes Umeshu with the fruit she harvests from the tree in her front yard. While always unfailingly generous with the current year's bounty, for a truly special occasion she'll pull back the rug in the dining room, open up the cellar door hidden beneath, and pull out one of the bottles that have been steeping for decades.

A note about Ume: Often erroneously called "Japanese plums" ume are, in fact, Japanese apricots.

A note about Umeshu: I drink it for its taste! But some people drink Umeshu for its medicinal properties, reported to soothe sore throats, ease indigestion and stimulate one's appetite.

A note about Shochu: The method for making Umeshu involves steeping ume in *shochu*—a potent, distilled spirit that, depending on where it's produced, can be made from such diverse vegetables or grains as potato, sweet potato, rice, barley and buckwheat.

Sometimes referred to as Japanese vodka, shochu is commonly drunk on the rocks, mixed with hot water, or mixed with soda water and/or fresh squeezed juice and served as *chuhai*—a cocktail especially popular with Japanese women.

I n early spring, even before the fêted cherry blossoms arrive, *ume*, the white Japanese apricot blossoms, color the landscape. A few months later, the trees bear fruit and grocery stores all over Japan are filled with supplies for making *umeboshi* (salt-pickled Japanese apricots) and *Umeshu* (Japanese apricot liqueur). As the saying goes, "Gently wiping a green ume clean—a sign that summer has begun." Although you can buy commercially made Umeshu all

Japanese Shisho Liqueur
Shisoshu

MAKES ABOUT 2 LITERS (8 CUPS)

3 lbs (1¹/₃ kg) fresh Japanese apricots (ume) of roughly equal size
7¾ cups (1³/₄ liters) shochu
2 lbs (1 kg) rock sugar (kori zato)

1. Wash and thoroughly dry the Japanese apricots. Remove any remaining stems with the tip of a toothpick.
2. To sterilize the container, pour a small amount of shochu on a paper towel and wipe clean the inside and around the lip.
3. Gently add the Japanese apricots, one at a time, so as not to bruise.
4. Pour in the shochu.
5. Add the rock sugar.
6. Seal the container tightly, write the date on the lid, and let steep in a cool, dark place for a minimum of 3 months, gently swirling every couple of weeks. If you haven't consumed the batch after 1 year, strain out the Japanese apricots to keep the liquid from becoming cloudy. (But don't throw out the steeped apricots. Eat them! They're delicious.)
7. Serve chilled over ice.

Umeshu Tips *When making* Umeshu, *there is no need to splurge on expensive shochu. When the Japanese apricots (ume) are in season, you'll find the liquor used for making Umeshu sold in paperboard cartons in the produce section of Japanese grocery stores.*

Also likely in close vicinity will be the rock sugar and handy containers for making and storing the finished Umeshu.

While some people will start drinking Umeshu 1 month after making, it is best to let the Japanese apricots steep a minimum of 3 months before enjoying.

Special Equipment *Large glass or plastic container with tight-fitting screw-top lid*

Whenever I think of Ikuko, it's her *shochu* infusions I'm reminded of. Anytime I happen to stop over for a visit—day or night—she's sure to offer me a sample of her latest concoction. Of course, her knowing how highly I think of her libations helps to give added weight to her heavy-handed pours!

One Sunday late in June, Hitomi and I went over to Ikuko's house to help prepare that year's batch of Japanese Apricot Liqueur (see recipe at left). While washing the just-picked Japanese apricots (*ume*), Ikuko gave us each a small glass of her latest infusion to try: *Shisoshu*. Although the first sip is almost unbearable in its unfamiliarity—a spicy taste with a tingly, numbing feeling reminiscent of the herb itself—you strangely find yourself coming back for more. As we drank, Ikuko kept asking if we could feel the herb's heat in the back of our throats? All I felt was buzzed!

Shiso is available year round, but Ikuko typically makes this infusion in June when she makes her annual batch of Japanese Apricot Liqueur.

MAKES ABOUT 2 LITERS (8 CUPS)

80 to 100 green shiso leaves (aojiso)
1 lemon, peeled and cut in half or thirds
½ lb (250 g) rock sugar (kori zato) or ½ to 1 cup (125 to 250 ml) honey
7¾ cups (1¾ liters) shochu

1. Gently rinse the shiso leaves and pat dry, being careful not to bruise.
2. To sterilize the container, pour a small amount of *shochu* on a paper towel and wipe clean the inside and around the lip.
3. Add the shiso, lemon and honey, if using.
4. Pour in the shochu.
5. Add the rock sugar, if using.
6. Seal the container tightly, write the date on the lid, and let steep in a cool, dark place for a minimum of 3 months, gently swirling every couple of weeks. If you haven't consumed the batch after one year, strain out the Japanese apricots to keep the liquid from becoming cloudy. (But don't throw out the steeped apricots. Eat them! They're delicious.)
7. Serve chilled over ice.

Special Equipment *Large glass or plastic container with tight-fitting screw-top lid*

Japanese Teas

Because of Japan, I am now addicted to green tea. There is rarely a day that goes by where I don't start the morning with a cup of the hot, bitter liquid. I love the taste, as well as the sentiment it embodies. Whether you're visiting a shop, a *ryokan* (traditional Japanese inn) or the home of your best friend, you're oftentimes welcomed with a freshly brewed cup of grassy green tea, an invitation to relax and converse.

Sencha

Genmaicha

Bancha

How to Brew a Cup of Tea

1. Bring the water to a boil, and then let cool to the temperature preferred for the specific type of tea leaves you are brewing—this helps preserve the tea's delicate flavor. A thermometer is the best judge, but a less scientific method is to simply wait about 5 minutes after boiling.

2. Before adding the tea leaves, add hot water to the tea pot and serving cups. Swirl to heat the vessels evenly, and then pour out.

3. As a general rule, use 1 tablespoon tea leaves for every 1 cup (250 ml) of water, plus one additional tablespoon for the pot. See the Tea Chart, page 155, for specific amounts and steeping times.

4. To serve the tea, pour a small amount of tea into each teacup, continuing to pour in "batches" until the teapot is empty. This helps ensure each person receives the same strength tea.

Japanese Tea Tips

• As a general rule, higher-quality teas should be brewed for shorter amounts of time and at lower temperatures to preserve their delicate and nuanced flavors.

• When steeping tea leaves, you can use hotter water for the second and third steeping.

• Green tea is never served with milk, sugar, or lemon. If made from a tea bag, it is never served with the tea bag still steeping in the cup.

• The longer you let tea steep, the stronger— and especially when it comes to green tea—the more bitter and astringent it will become.

• Store tea in an airtight container in a cool, dry place. Although some suggest otherwise, do not store tea in the freezer—it can act as baking soda does, taking on the different aromas from the freezer.

• Tea's shelf life is similar to that of spices'. For the most part, tea never really goes "bad." It just loses its flavor intensity over time. That said, there are certain teas you will want to consume within a year or two. Japanese green and white teas, for example, are generally harvested from smaller leaf varietals and are minimally processed so the flavor profile can diminish quickly. Conversely, there are others such as oolong and pu-erh teas that only get better with age!

Tea Terminology

O-cha—General name for all tea. *Cha* means "tea," but the word is seldom used alone. Instead, the honorific "O" usually precedes it.

Ryokucha—General name for all green teas.

Green Teas

Gyokuro—Highest quality green tea leaves. Expensive. Same leaves used to make *matcha*. Water's color after steeping is a very pale green. Least bitter and astringent of the green teas. Enjoyed in small servings, often with *wagashi* (traditional Japanese sweet).

Sencha—Very nice mid-range tea. Served for both formal occasions and everyday enjoyment. Different grades of *sencha* are determined by the degree of steaming and season harvested.

Kukicha

Hojicha

Matcha

Hojicha—Roasted *bancha*. Has less caffeine than other green teas. Often enjoyed after a meal, especially dinner. Good to pair with oily foods.

Kukicha—A less expensive variety of green tea comprising twigs and older tea leaves. Less bitter and astringent than *sencha*.

Bancha—Lower quality green tea made from older leaves and stems. Less caffeine. Everyday tea. The lower the grade of *bancha*, the more twigs and stems included. Turns bitter when cold; serve warm.

Genmaicha—Also called "popcorn tea." *Sencha* or *bancha* with roasted rice or rice cracker granules. Less caffeine.

Matcha (also called hikicha)—Powdered green tea made from *gyokuro* tea leaves. Most commonly used in formal tea ceremonies. Bright jade color. Also great for cooking, making ice creams or adding to cake batter, for example.

Other Teas

Sobacha—Roasted buckwheat tea. Beautiful sweet, nutty flavor with a very distinct aroma wonderfully reminiscent of Japan. Caffeine-free. Water's color turns light brown after steeping. As it's not a traditional tea, the brewing process is much less restricted—no tea leaves to worry about damaging. Pour just-boiled water over *sobacha* nibs—about 1 tablespoon per 1 cup (250 ml) water—and let steep about 5 minutes. The greater the nibs-to-water ratio, as well as the longer it's steeped, the stronger the tea. The crunchy sobacha nibs can also be cooked with—try adding to cookie dough or as a topping on ice cream.

Mugicha—Roasted barely tea. Where America has its sweet tea and its lemonade, Japan has its *mugicha*. During the hot summer months, freshly brewed mugicha is a staple in every Japanese home—served over ice, it's a necessary means for keeping oneself cool. To brew, simply drop a tea bag into a pitcher of cold water and steep in the refrigerator for 30 minutes.

"Kiddy" Cocktail—When I went to visit a friend in Niigata, on the western coast of Japan, he told me how, when he was young, his mom would add a little bit of Japanese Apricot Liqueur (see recipe, page 152) to his mugicha. Although the combination seems a bit inappropriate for a child, it is a tasty way to give some kick to barley tea.

Tea Chart

Listed below is a chart for brewing different types of green tea. Use the temperatures provided only as a starting point. The best temperature for each type of tea may vary slightly depending on the grade of the tea leaves you are using.

Tea	Water Temperature	Tea Leaves: Water Ratio	Steeping Time
Gyokuro	165°F (75°C)	1 tb per 8 oz	3 minutes
Sencha	180°F (82°C)	1 tsp per 8 oz	3 to 4 minutes
Hojicha	185°F (85°C)	1 tb per 8 oz	3 to 4 minutes
Kukicha	185°F (85°C)	1 tb per 8 oz	3 to 4 minutes
Bancha	185°F (85°C)	1 tb per 8 oz	3 to 4 minutes
Genmaicha	180°F (82°C)	1 tsp per 8 oz	2 to 3 minutes
Matcha	175°F (80°C)	1½ tsp. per 4 to 5 oz.	Whisk with *chasen* (traditional bamboo whisk) until dissolved and frothy
Sobacha	Boiling hot	1 tb per 8 oz	5 minutes
Mugicha	Cold	1 bag per 1 L/ 1 quart pitcher	30 minutes

Acknowledgments

There is a saying in Japanese, "*Ichi-go, Ichi-e,*" which, loosely translated means a magical moment in time, never to be recreated, but only visited in memory. Working on this book has been that magical time for me. The experiences, the challenges, the people (many of whom were strangers) that helped me along the way . . . I truly feel the stars were aligned.

I could not have done this without you. Thank you . . .

Brad, for giving me the idea I could write a book in the first place.

Ladd, for inspiring me to create something of my own.

Mikiko Komatsu, for hiring me at your English school and bringing me to Iwaki.

April (my sister), for first introducing me to Hitomi.

My Japanese family, my home away from home: Hitomi, Hideaki, Hinao & Masashi Ono; Hiromi Matsumoto; Toyozou, Takako & Noriko Ishikura; Hideo & Ikuko Ono. The love and generosity you have given me, the experiences you created and included me in . . . it is because of you that Japan is forever a part of me.

Contributors, without you there would be no book. Literally. Irohado Oyaki Shop (Kinasa); Takeko Kubohara (and daughters Mari & Yukari); Obuse Guide Center—especially Etsuko Seki & Reiko Toyoda; The Hemmis (Atsuko, Hikaru, Raito, Rei, & Kei); Tono Youth Hostel; Manchan Coffee Shop (Hirosaki); Hideo & the Moya Kogen Youth Hostel; Uonuma Association for Multicultural Exchange—especially Sekia-san, Banzai-san & Masashi Watanabe; Takamatsu Goodwill Guides—especially Narita Shohachiro, Shizuka Maruura & Hiroko Miyoshi; Etsuko Itami, Ayako Sakaguchi & their generous family; Ehime Prefectural International Centre—especially director Motoyuki Wada,

coordinator Noriko Omori and the wonderful fisherman Katsuji Shigekawa; Matsuyama Youth Hostel; Michiko Nagata & Shizuka Kumamaru; Satsuma-Aji Chef (Ibusuki); Junbo Café (Kagoshima); Ayano Naruoka and her parents Nobuyuki and Kazuyo.

Recipe Testers, for making these recipes taste and work better than I could have ever done on my own: Paul Feldner (my dad!); Sue Hoss (a fantastic baker and all-around great cook); John McMillan & Elizabeth Russell; Debra Shapiro; mother-daughter-duo Nancy & Gretchen Kern; Trish Iaccarino; Lizz Fabel; Sarah Buckley; Mandy Lindbergh; Amy Fry & Robert Ray; Amy Cassell & Sarah Bissen; Signe Knudsen; Linda Bunger; Susan Fey; Nichole Abresch; Brad Dumville (proving that even a vegan can enjoy this book!).

Susana Mojica and everyone at Rishi Tea, for helping me muddle my way through all the wonderful nuances of Japanese green tea.

Allison Silver Adelman, for all your translating services. Especially when you thought you were long-finished with this project, and then I kept coming back with one "last-minute" question after another.

Elizabeth Andoh, for answering my out-of-the-blue email, a correspondence that evolved into your mentoring me through this cookbook project. Crazy how things work. Thank you!

Taeko Kamei at the Tuttle office in Tokyo and June Chong at the Periplus office in Singapore, for helping facilitate communication with the contributors and photography team, as well as handling a thousand other details.

Yumi Kawachi (food stylist), for successfully recreating these recipes in Japan, relieving my perfectionist anxiety and proving they really do work. You turned words on paper into beautiful, delicious results. Additional thanks to Natsuho Sugawa (cooking assistant).

Noboru Murata (photographer), for being as talented as you are. The overall aesthetic of this cookbook was as important to me as the recipes and stories. Thank you for listening to my vision and then turning it into something even better. Additional thanks to Tomoko Osada (assistant photographer) and Kaoru Murata (photo coordinator).

Chan Sow Yun (designer), for organizing all the components into this impressive package.

The Japanese store Grand Chef (2-18-15, Jiyugaoka, Megro-ku, Tokyo, Japan, 152-0035; Tel. 81-3-3724-8989; www.grandchef.co.jp) for lending kitchen tools and Rie Imai for lending dishware for the photography sessions.

Eric Oey (my publisher), for believing in this first-time author and helping bring my dream to a gorgeous, tangible reality.

Holly Jennings (my editor), for having patience while I got married, worked full time, wrote my monthly column, bought a house and attempted to maintain some sort of social life . . . all while trying to make this book the best I possibly could. Your detailed questions and edits frustrated and challenged me. The result was well worth it.

April and my very patient brother-in-law, Jesse, for allowing me to crash at your home in San Francisco for a couple of months(!) when I first got back from Japan until I figured out "what next?".

Rick (my step-dad), for expanding your creativity into the kitchen, allowing me to grow up in an environment where food was fun and beautiful and meant to be played with.

Paul Feldner (father-of-mine) and Laura Marx (mumzie), for always encouraging and supporting me along the many paths I've needed to explore. And for granting me as many opportunities as you have. I could never thank you enough for being the parents you are.

Kevin (my husband), for going through this lengthy process with me. We met when this book was already set in my mind, and the years of work that followed—the late nights, early mornings and entire weekends—took away from your time, as well. Thank you for waiting this out. I love you.

Suggested Menus

Summer Sampler
Gingerade, Cold Sesame Noodle Salad, Green Tea Snow Cone

Sushi Party
Pickled Ginger, Handrolled Sushi, Broiled Salmon, Green Tea Ice Cream with Black Sugar Syrup, Toasted Sesame Cookies

Weeknight Meal
Sesame Salad Dressing, Sesame-Seared Beef OR Soy-Glazed Chicken Wings, White Rice

Light Lunch
Fava Bean Soup, Crispy Rice Snacks

Picnic
Japanese Egg Salad Sandwiches, Crispy Buckwheat Cookies

Appetizer Party
Marinated Mushrooms, One-Bite Sushi Nibbles, Almond Rice Onigiri, Japanese Cocktail Peanuts, Yakitori Chicken Skewers

Casual Dinner Party
White Radish Salad, Braised Spare Ribs, Spicy Carrot and Burdock Root, Banana Chiffon Cake

For the Newly Initiated
Udon Soup with Chicken Meatballs, Fried Soba Noodles and Rice, Sugared Bread Sticks

Vegan
Mixed Tofu Soup, Fried Potatoes with Miso and Sesame, Green Tea

Potluck-Ready
Five Color Salad, Sushi Rice with Toppings

Rice Toppers
Eggplant Miso, Hitomi's Rice Topping, Fresh Eggplant Rice Topper

Resource Guide

Fresh & dried produce
Diamond Organics
www.diamondorganics.com

Earthy Delights
www.earthy.com

Melissa's
www.melissas.com

Grow your own
Kitazawa Seed Company
www.kitazawaseed.com

For all your instant noodle needs
Ramen Depot
www.ramendepot.com

Miso
Miso Master Organic Miso
www.great-eastern-sun.com
Available online and at select grocers

South River Miso
www.southrivermiso.com
Available online and at select grocers

Tofu & yuba
Hodo Soy Beanery
www.hodosoy.com

Online grocers
Amazon.com
www.amazon.com

Asian Food Grocer
www.asianfoodgrocer.com

Pacific Rim Gourmet
www.pacificrimgourmet.com
Japanese ingredients section

If you're in the neighborhood—Japanese grocers
Mitsuwa
California, Chicago, New Jersey
www.mitsuwa.com

Nijiya
California, Hawaii, New York
www.nijiya.com

Uwajimaya
Pacific Northwest
www.uwajimaya.com

Tea
Rishi Tea
www.rishi-tea.com
Available online and at select grocers

Beer
Kiuichi Brewery
Makers of Hitachino Nest Beer
www.kodawari.cc
Available at select grocers and liquor stores

Equipment
Korin
www.korin.com
Japanese knives, kitchen utensils and tableware

Natural wasabi powder
Penzeys Spices
www.penzeys.com
Available online and at Penzeys stores across the country.

The Spice House
www.thespicehouse.com
Retail stores in Chicago and Milwaukee areas. Great Web site, with photos, detailed descriptions and accompanying recipes.

And if you ever find yourself in Wauwatosa, Wisconsin, be sure to stop in at the spice shop on Glenview Avenue, where you'll find William and Ruth Penzey—the proud parents of the Penzey-family spice empire.

Index

The recipe for green tea ice cream (see Green Tea Ice Cream with Black Sugar Syrup, page 148) was reprinted with permission from *Washoku* by Elizabeth Andoh. Copyright 2005 by Elizabeth Andoh, Ten Speed Press, Berkeley, CA. www.tenspeed.com

Published by Tuttle Publishing, an imprint of Periplus Editions (HK) Ltd., with editorial offices at 364 Innovation Drive, North Clarendon, Vermont 05759 U.S.A. and 61 Tai Seng Avenue, #02-12, Singapore 534167

Library of Congress Cataloging-in-Publication Data

Feldner, Sarah Marx.
A cook's journey to Japan: fish tales and rice paddies: 100 homestyle recipes from Japanese kitchens / Sarah Marx Feldner; photography by Noboru Murata; styling by Yumi Kawachi.
    p. cm.
  Includes index.
  ISBN 978-4-8053-1011-3 (hardcover)
  1. Cookery, Japanese. 2. Cookery–Japan. I. Title.
  TX724.5.J3F45 2010
  641.5951--dc22
                    2009031566

ISBN 978-4-8053-1011-3

Distributed by
North America, Latin America & Europe
Tuttle Publishing
364 Innovation Drive
North Clarendon, VT 05759-9436 U.S.A.
Tel: 1 (802) 773-8930
Fax: 1 (802) 773-6993
info@tuttlepublishing.com
www.tuttlepublishing.com

Japan
Tuttle Publishing
Yaekari Building, 3rd Floor
5-4-12 Osaki, Shinagawa-ku, Tokyo 141 0032
Tel: (81) 3 5437-0171
Fax: (81) 3 5437-0755
tuttle-sales@gol.com

Asia Pacific
Berkeley Books Pte. Ltd.
61 Tai Seng Avenue #02-12
Singapore 534167
Tel: (65) 6280-1330
Fax: (65) 6280-6290
inquiries@periplus.com.sg
www.periplus.com

12 11 10   10 9 8 7 6 5 4 3 2 1
Printed in Singapore

TUTTLE PUBLISHING® is a registered trademark of Tuttle Publishing, a division of Periplus Editions (HK) Ltd.

HOKKAIDŌ

Sapporo

HONSHU

Aomori

Hirosaki

Morioka

Akita

Tono

Yamagata

Niigata

Fukushima

Aizu-Wakamatsu

Uonuma

Iwaki

Kinasa · Obuse

Hotaka · Nagano

Matsumoto

Kasumigaura
Lake

Fukui

Tsukuba

Kyōto

Nagoya

TOKYO

Kobe

Okayama

Hiroshima

Takamatsu

Osaka

Kotohira

*Oboke
Gorge*

Tokushima

Fukuoka

Matsuyama

Kochi

*Shimanto
Gawa River*

Yufuin

SHIKOKU

Uwajima

Kumamoto

KYUSHU

Miyazaki

Kagoshima

Ibusuki

*R y u k y u   I s l a n d s
(O k i n a w a)*

Amami-Ōshima

Okinawa-jima

Okinawa